The Phoenix and The Poet

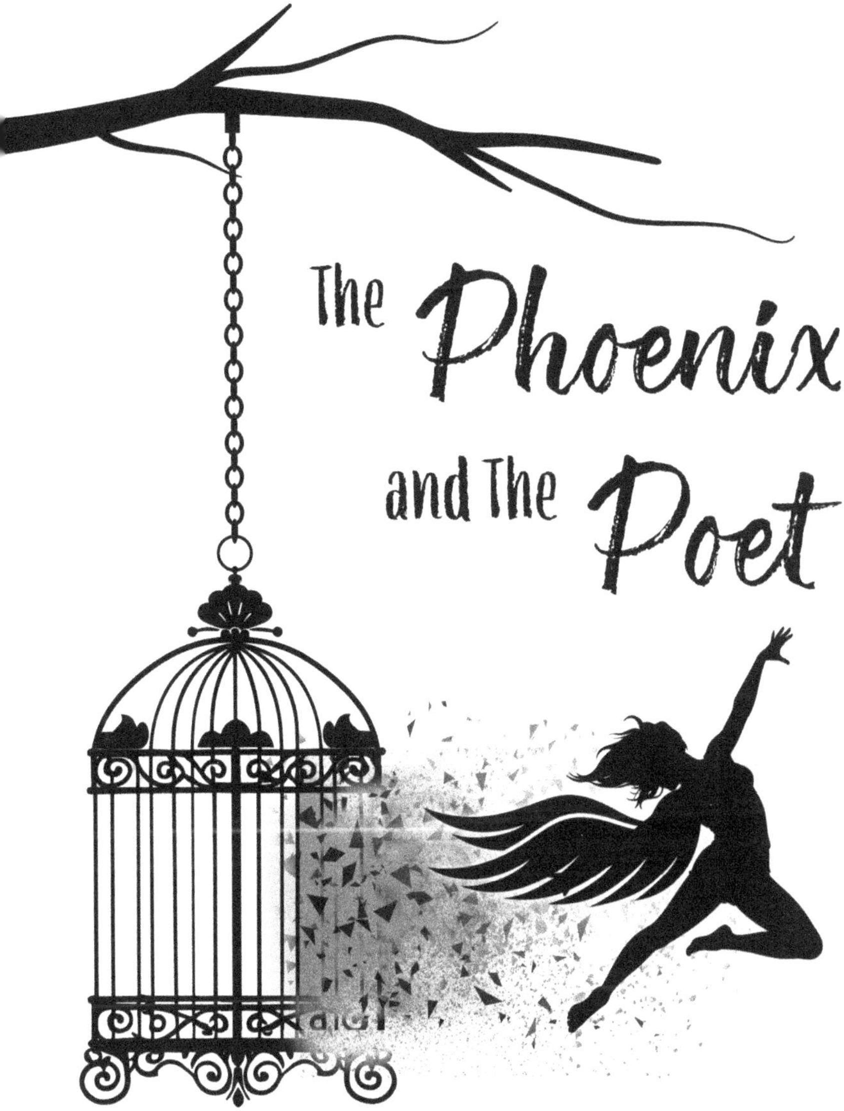

The *Phoenix*
and The *Poet*

Poems of Fire, Faith, and Transformation

Wendy Koury

Farmhouse
Publishings

For information on distribution rights, royalties, derivative works, or licensing opportunities on behalf of this content or work, please contact the publisher at the address below:

Farmhouse Publishings, LLC
P.O. Box 333
Spearfish, SD 57783

Scripture quotations taken from the Holy Bible, New International Version ®, NIV ® Copyright © 1973, 1978, 1984, 2011 by Biblica, Inc. Used with permission. All rights reserved worldwide. Scripture quotations are from the Revised Standard Version of the Bible, Copyright © 1946, 1952, and 1971 the Division of Christian Education of the National Council of the Churches of Christ in the United States of America. Used by permission. All rights reserved.

ISBN (Hardcover):979-8-9996472-9-0
ISBN (Softcover): 979-8-9996472-2-1
ISBN (Ebook): 979-8-9996472-3-8

Design by Heidi Caperton
Cover Design by Heidi Caperton and Deja Miller

Printed in the United States of America

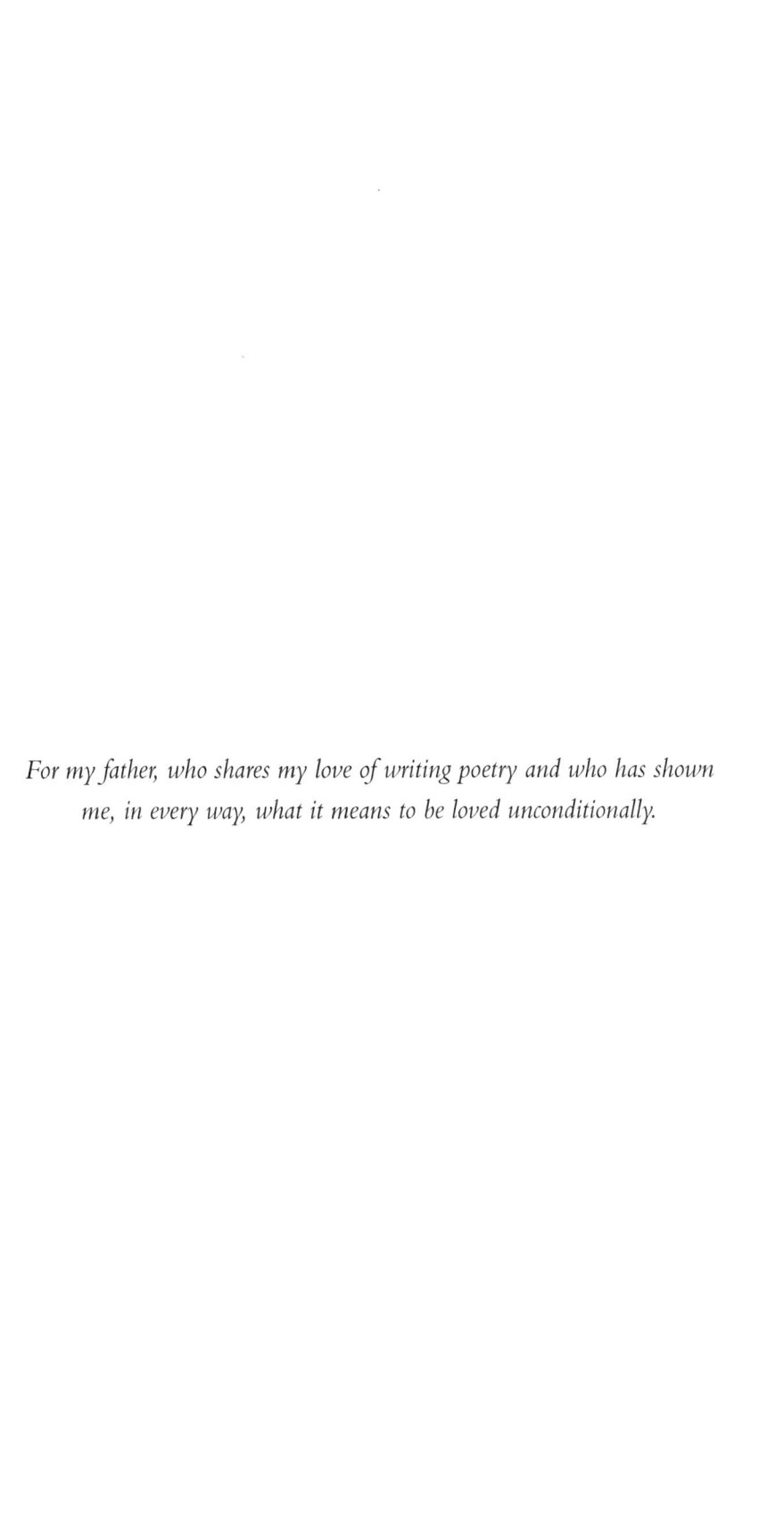

For my father, who shares my love of writing poetry and who has shown me, in every way, what it means to be loved unconditionally.

Contents

Chapter Three: Spirituality and Faith   45

Chapter Four: Life's Challenges and Struggles   59

Chapter Eight: Discovering Purpose   129

Forward

Poetry has the extraordinary power to speak to the soul, weaving words into feelings, moments, and truths that transcend time. Poetry serves as a mirror, reflecting our joys, struggles and everything in between, while also acting as a lantern, guiding us toward understanding, compassion, and hope. *The Phoenix and the Poet* does all of this and more. This collection invites you on a soulful journey, one that will touch the profound corners of your heart while awakening the quiet strength often tucked away in life's shadows.

At the heart of this collection is the phoenix: an enduring symbol of transformation and resilience. Like this mythical creature, the poems rise from the ashes of hardship, loss and doubt, offering not only survival but rebirth. Alongside the phoenix is the poet, a figure who artfully captures the complexity of life, transforming it into verse that encourages introspection and connection. Together, they create a harmony of resilience and creativity, a partnership that reminds us of our own capacity to grow and evolve.

This book is divided into thematic chapters that echo the natural rhythm of life itself. Through its pages, you will celebrate milestones and triumphs, explore the depth of love, and find courage in the face of adversity. The poems call you to pause, to breathe and to reflect on the beauty and truth embedded in the everyday—the sunrise, a shared laugh, a small but meaningful choice. And as you move through its final chapters, grounding yourself in faith, you'll be encouraged to seek the wisdom and purpose that comes from looking within.

There is a vulnerability in these poems that draws us close. The words resonate because they are universal. They are our stories, reimagined into lines of verse. The grief of loss, the joy of a connection found, the quiet strength of perseverance.

Each theme carries an emotional weight we've all known. And yet, every poem also offers hope, a reminder of the invincible spirit we hold within ourselves.

What makes *The Phoenix and the Poet* so remarkable is its invitation to all of us. You don't need to be a seasoned poetry reader to feel its impact. These poems are for anyone willing to slow down and engage with life's questions. The poems challenge us to look inward and examine who we are, while simultaneously inspiring us to build and rebuild the life we envision. It is not a book you read once and set aside. *The Phoenix and the Poet* is one to return to, time and again, to draw courage, to revisit forgotten parts of yourself, or simply to be reminded of the light that persists even in darkness.

Whether you are here to seek solace, discover new perspectives, or simply lose yourself in words, this collection has something to offer. Its pages carry the essence of humanity, fragile, flawed, yet unimaginably beautiful. Through these poems, we are reminded that no matter how the flames of life may burn us, there is always the potential to rise again, stronger and brighter than before.

As you hold this book in your hands, I invite you to open your heart fully. Step into the world these poems create, allow their themes to guide you, and remain open to the truths they reveal. You may emerge from these pages changed, with a clearer understanding of life's complexity and an even greater appreciation for its resilience.

Remember, like the phoenix, we are all capable of rising. Like the poet, we are all storytellers of our own lives. This collection honors those truths and reminds us of the strength and beauty that emerge when we dare to look within, to love boldly, and to persevere.

Welcome to *The Phoenix and the Poet*. May it bring you insights, inspiration and, above all, hope.

XOXO

Deja ♡

Chapter One

Life Lessons and Growth

This chapter explores self-discovery, resilience and learning through life's trials. Poems like *Living Our Best* inspire authenticity, while *Faith* showcases strength drawn from belief.

Symbolic works like *What's in Your Backpack* focus on managing life's burdens, and *Perfect Vision* highlights growth through shifting perceptions. Together, the poems encourage transformation and breaking limiting patterns.

Living Our Best

Living fully authentic, I'm sure we think we do
But are there circumstances when this may not be true?
Do we change ourselves for others in an effort to fit in
Do we portray a different image than what's underneath our skin?

Do we want to be with people that society says are cool?
If we act how we would like, to all of them we'd be a fool
So instead of seeking out the friends we would align
We make ourselves feel less-than, dim our light so it won't shine

Are we a different person when at work as we compete?
As we fight to make our way, to succeed, to be elite
And do we suppress pieces that may not help us with this goal
Do we think it is okay to hide any part of our own soul?

To be authentic sounds so easy, but it can come at quite a cost
The people you share time with, from your life they may be lost
As you align yourself, to act and speak what's in your heart
The new "you" they thought they knew, may cause them to depart

To be genuine is worth it, even though a price is paid
For it will bring new people, a new foundation will be laid
And if they all are focused on the truth and love around
The life you will have made will show blessings that abound

So go ahead and be authentic; your gut will guide the way
Stay fast in your own power, in alignment try to stay
Don't apologize to others for being who you are
Your happiness will thank you and you will shine like a bright star

The light that it will cast may illuminate the road
For others who are struggling and carrying a load
To help another person is what we're here to do
So let us be authentic, and to ourselves let's all be true

Faith

Have you ever climbed a mountain and found yourself at what felt like a dead end? You may stand at the edge of this cliff viewing the green hills, animals and flowers on the other side. A gorge stands between the two. You may think, *my ability to move forward is halted by this sudden change in land mass.* But is it?

What if the cliff you are standing on, holds all your wants. It's a big cliff. Many of us want a lot but fail to appreciate the solid ground we are currently standing on. And what if the green hills on the other side represent what we get to have or receive. How do we bridge this gorge to open ourselves up to these gifts?

First, we need to believe we are worthy of this adventure. Next, we need to see the bridge that takes us from one side to the next. Can you feel how it would feel to be on that bridge and reach the other side, to receive what you so long for? Finally, you need to take the first step forward confidently. It's important to not get swept up into fear, as that mindset will only let you see the bridge that is not attached on the other side or the depth of the gorge, and you will feel stuck like your feet are bound and unable to move.

Gratitude for what you currently have will help you with your focus Faith over fear is a real thing. The choice is yours.

What's in Your Backpack

Imagine being fitted with a backpack at our birth
It's invisible but present, as we walk along through earth
All that we experience, and the memories that they hold
Are added to the backpack as our lives start to unfold

Now memories can be clouded by how we choose to see
Their impact can be good or bad, and will grow just like a tree
Some memories that we add will feel light and full of joy
Some will feel like weights, our ease they do destroy

People will all walk with different postures to be sure
Their packs may be quite heavy; they seek but find no cure
They do not realize that there's a choice that they can make
That will ease all that they carry, on the steps they choose to take

You see the very memories that we put into our pack
Weren't meant to hold us down, reveal all that we do lack
The lightest ones should stay under the zipper that secures.
The heavy ones remove; they only take you on detours

And as you journey on, how will you start to see your life
If you change your way of thinking, you'll find value in the strife
The things that you do conquer, build your self-esteem for sure
They help you climb the stairs, always worth what we endure

So whether you rise up from all the lightness in your pack
Or from slowly trudging up, each stair that you attack
Keep a mindful eye; don't get stuck with heavy packs
Keep moving towards the light, your shoulders will relax

The lightness you will feel, will be quite obvious if you do
And the bricks you place before you, aid the road you will pursue
Both can be of service; it depends on what you choose
Does your pack help lift you up, or extinguish your life's fuse

Weeding Out Our Thoughts

It happens in the spring, its bloom one of the first
A welcome sign to bees, for nectar they do thirst
The full round yellow bloom, appears just like the sun
It closes up at night when the day is nearly done

Salad can be made with its leaves if we so choose
The flowers can make wine, or tea if one so brews
Before its life is over, one more gift it does supply
A rounded puff of seedlings, to blow off and say goodbye

A wish can then be made as they carry in the breeze
And if the wish is granted, life may grant a bit of ease
Its life is oh-so-simple, yet it carries beauty, too
To be appreciated, I understand it is by few

Yet this is God's creation, just like many we admire
It's funny how its beauty, we've been taught to not desire
We're trained to call the dandelion, nothing but a weed
From what other ways of thinking do our minds need to be freed?

Perfect Vision

I have an important job to do today. I have been selected to bring new eyeglasses to the people in the next village. The glasses are loaded up in my satchel in cases that will protect them. These people have been through a lot, and it will be great to supply something to improve their vision. I gladly accept the task.

Martha has suffered the loss of her husband this year. She has no children, and her dog is old and ailing.

William was let go from his job. He filed for bankruptcy and lost his home and way of life.

Sharon is recovering from an abusive, alcoholic father. She was in foster care much of her life.

Michael is suffering from a debilitating auto-immune disorder.

As I head out on this journey with only my thoughts, I think back on my life. Gratitude, love and my faith have guided me on my path. Much like the people of this village, I've had my fair share of challenges. We all will. I reflect on how I made it through those challenges, what I have learned and how it changed the way I saw and tackled new things that I experienced.

Up ahead, I see something but can't quite see the details as I have forgotten MY glasses today. I reach into the satchel to borrow a pair. As I put each of them on, it's strange as I observe a different upcoming view.

Martha and William's glasses show a steep, winding hill ahead with many rocks to crawl over. On the horizon, I see a dark moon. This trail appears bleak and hopeless with nothing to look forward to at the end.

Sharon and Michael's glasses reveal only a slight incline on this trail with fragrant flowers along the way. A beautiful sunrise is evident at the end of the destination.

As I reflect on their lives now, I see Martha has not met any new friends in life, has stopped going to book club and has continued to isolate away. William has let the words of his boss define his life. He has not searched for his talents, but instead remains living on the street.

While Sharon has married a very caring man, is a foster mom and continues to be active in Al-Anon. Michael sought out alternative healthcare and his health has improved. He started a non-profit to continue helping others with the same misfortune.

I ponder on what I have experienced with all their glasses. It seems each of them has experienced setbacks in life. Some have chosen to stay stuck and see the upcoming world darkly while others have used those challenges as steppingstones and are excited for what lies ahead. I find compassion in my heart as I put each pair on, realizing what they each have lived through and how they now see life.

I believe we each should look through another's glasses occasionally as we would judge less. We may understand how their experiences shaped their vision. That being said, it is equally important to realize that we all have choices that will have future repercussions. When I arrive, I will place the glasses on a table and have them find their own. I'm hoping what they experience trying each other's on will be as eye opening as it was for me.

Rebirth

The tree has fallen in the woods, no one around to hear
Its purpose redirected, for animals that live near
Its nutrients will return, to the soil from which it came
New plants begin to grow, and some will live within its frame

The fire moves so quickly, through the forest it does spread
The people watch with horror, the final outcome they so dread
But does it just destroy, or is there healing to be found
Seeds are heated and crack open, new life is within the ground

The diamond we desire, has a story to reveal
We don't witness its creation, just the outcome and appeal
It endured high temps and pressure, and came out a better thing
We'd be wise to be like diamonds; the lesson does so ring

There are things that happen throughout life, that seem to just destroy
When we focus on the loss and hurt, we lose our sense of joy
And know that all things beautiful, have taken this similar path
We don't see the things that they've been through, we just see the aftermath

I may seem to have it all, and I agree I'm truly blessed
My gratitude runs deep, and in God's arms I surely rest
There are things that near destroyed me, but they planted a new seed
Just because you didn't witness, doesn't mean I didn't bleed

So judge me not for who I am, or how my life is going
We've all been given oars, in the stream that we are rowing
I've long ago thrown victimhood, over the side of my life boat
It made my load much lighter, further downstream I trust I'll float

We all decide how we view, the hurts that life dishes up
Is your glass half full or empty, as you pour from your life's cup?

An Uphill Climb

Imagine life a mountain with an upward path we climb
It winds around from north to east, then south to west in time
As we round the bend with each, we will come to understand
Each side gives us new lessons; in our life they all will land

Life may feel a bit windy as we start out in the north
But then we see the east sunrise and know we can move forth
Then comes along the heat in life as we round the southern bend
The sunset on the western side makes our day feel on the mend.

The inclination varies, sometimes flat can change to steep
There are ones who walk beside us and their company we keep
The path is made of dirt and rock, grassy patches we will find
Our feet may feel the softened earth and the mud our boots won't mind

We may walk beside a friend or two along a widened part
The narrow paths we face alone may seem scary as we start
As we look at those quite high above on this path that is a must
A harness can be seen on them, like a life net they can trust

They made it past the puddles, ledges, temps, and the rough rock
The harness helped to ease the storms when the darkness came to knock
To have them reach and pull us up to prevent our painful sections
Will rob us from our chance to learn even with our imperfections

We will come across some people, worn down and out of luck
They may choose to reverse course or settle down in all the muck
Keep moving on around these souls, say a prayer as you move past
And grab your harness tighter, the pain in life won't last

If we keep moving on and up, we'll reach the very top
The memories and the love we shared just continue and don't stop
And the view that we now see is beyond imagination
As we hand the harness back to God and thank Him for our creation.

Are you Curious?

"Curiosity killed the cat," is how the saying goes
"But satisfaction brought it back," is the next line no one knows
It's meant to cause some fear, when we challenge status quo
But the risk just might be worth it; where it leads to, minds may blow

When children are quite young, they hit a certain stage
Where all they ask is "why" as their learning does engage
To question what we know and reach for understanding
Allows our world to grow, to arrive at a new landing

In medicine and science, religion and history
A question is required to unlock the mystery
What will we uncover as we dig into the facts
What new discoveries, brought to our life impacts

To never want to learn, or to halt its strong progression
Will cause all growth in life, to arrive at a regression
And there will be a lot who don't want for us to ask
But I believe for us, it is a fundamental task

So, I will choose to question and be curious in my life
To continue educating, even though it may cause strife
And though I do not have nine lives as the cats do
I'll have lived the one I have, seeking growth and what is true

Embrace the Shed

If you've ever owned a pet, you look past the loss of hair
They seem to shed a lot, with our vacuums we do share
And just because they shed, doesn't mean we love them less
It's all a part of growing, its purpose can't suppress

We see other living things, that follow in this way
Snakes and lizards shed their skin, hermit crabs old shells don't stay
The birds do lose their feathers; with the seasons change they molt
The caterpillar finds its wings, from the chrysalis it does bolt

The chick lost its protection, as it pecked its way on out
The shell was shed, now useless as it moves its wings about
And if you live up north, in the fall, enjoy the trees
The colors are magnificent, and with winter, loss of leaves

And humans also play in this shedding as we grow
We lose our baby teeth, new ones come from down below
Our skin cells, we lose thousands, as we move about our day
Our hair falls out, and tears are shed when emotions are at play

I feel that there is more to shed, in another area we grow
We need to question thoughts, beliefs, and everything we know
And look at other people, you walk with in this life
Some are lost to destiny, invite others out if strife

For shedding is quite necessary; it means new growth has come
Many grow quite quickly, but slower journeys are for some
Embrace your growth in life, challenge all parts of your being
Continue to change glasses, understand what you are seeing

Be happy for the shed, as it means we have evolved
To witness and address, another problem has been solved
But know that growth is painful, it may challenge you a bit
It's better than not changing, your new clothes are sure to fit

Eyes of the Wise

Through life we do all grow, it requires new skin to fit
As our size does seem to increase, and new beliefs we do permit
To evolve is not an option, it truly is a must
Our old selves break away, and our shells do start to bust

The snake loses its skin, it's discarded by the way
The significance it carried, no longer it will stay
The dermis it now wears, looks all shiny, bright and new
But the messages it carries, are still words that prove not true

Let us not keep focus on the old skin that was lost
Or the new one that presented, the solution sure to cost
But on the simple fact, that the snake is still a snake
No matter its exterior, false promises it will make

Its coat is not important, though it can look mighty fine
It's what it truly stands for, not how much it proves to shine
That we need to comprehend, before we fall into its lair
And lose our sense of self, life from our souls will tear

Fool me once, shame on you
Fool me twice, shame on me
Requires us all to see the snake
If you want a life that's truly free

Chapter Two

Relationships and Connections

*T*his chapter celebrates the connections that shape us. *Who's in Your Car?* examines the influence of the people we allow into our lives, while *The Dance of Life* underscores choosing companions aligned with our values. Pieces like *Be the Light* emphasize supporting loved ones, and tributes like *Car Rides with Dad* honor meaningful relationships. These works reflect the richness of family, friends, and shared love.

Who's in Your Car?

We've all loaded up a car, as the journey did begin
When we were young, we sat in back, next to our other kin
We functioned as a family, each type all represented
We learned things from each other, our personalities cemented

Then 16 years did pass, our own license we did get
One by one we left that car, our own journey we did set
We were free to give out rides, to anyone we chose
Not aware if these same people, were our friends or were our foes

They say that we're most like, the five we share our time
I'm hoping that your people, value out more than a dime
We will pick up many people, for each new phase of our life
Some will be our friends, others become husband or wife

Some will be professionals, we need for a mile or two
Some will teach us lessons, some may leave us feeling blue
Some stay in our car, present since we were quite young
Some will be much older, more living they have done

It's nice to be surrounded, by those most like ourselves
But invite some others in, new books they'll fill our shelves
And don't be that afraid, to let some out by the next block
It's good to understand, who in our tire will place a rock

Enjoy those in your car, who fill your trip with joy
And make the trials in life, fall away, the stress destroy
The copilot you choose, will have the biggest job
They'll warn of curves ahead, as to the music they will bob

And they will help you navigate, the roads to where you're going
They'll help prevent collisions, so your car will not need towing
Evaluate these people, in your life that you so choose
To ride along with you, as your journey so ensues

If I could recommend my co-pilot, I will share
I talk to Him quite often; some would call it but a prayer
My journey has been blessed, the storms we faced we did defeat
I think you've probably guessed, it is to God I give that seat

The Dance of Life

The date had been announced, the anticipation mounted
For the most important dance, as the days led up, we counted
And when it finally came, we dressed up in our best
We would rotate through the partners, our choice put through the test

The girls lined up in style, as they glanced at those to meet
Three sets of twins to choose from, let's hope with no left feet
Their last names clearly printed, on the front side of their shirt
But the backs held different verbiage, who they are it did alert

The first set of boys stepped forward, their last name labeled FEAR
On the back, Fear Everything And Run, and my first thought was, "Oh dear!"
The other one revealed, Face Everything And Rise
This is the kind of person that I'd like to harmonize

The next set of boys to dance with, a last name they called HATE
Hostility Against The Enemy, looked like love was all too late
The back side of the other, Help Anyone That Exists
I was happy when he came forward, led me to dance and took my wrists

The last set of boys presented, EGO was their known surname
The Even God Owes me brother, revealed the anger, what a shame
But the other one stepped forward with Everyone's Good Observed
He was what my soul did long for, and what I hoped I deserved

I noticed as I looked out on the ones, I met that day
It didn't matter their last names, that made me want to stay
But how their minds interpreted the lot they'd been assigned
I saw the differences that it made and how their life aligned

It didn't take us long, to know with whom we should align
The movements on the dance floor seemed to flow, almost divine
We silently did pray, for a match that was a fit
To dance the rest of life with, who our souls would then commit

In life we are most like, the partners we do choose
The dance was so enlightening, it left to us great clues
Evaluate your choices, the total circumstance
Be selective for your heart and soul, with whom you choose to dance

Be the Light

Our paths in this life merged, a candle each we did carry
As we walked on down the road, this chapter we would marry
Side by side we journeyed on, two lights better than my one
I welcomed in your company, as we watched the setting sun

My light began to grow, the candle does evolve
Into a mighty torch, as the darkness comes to call
Your candle also burned, but its brightness did not stay
It isn't competition, I just tried to light your way

False perceptions and assumptions, are like mud beneath my boots
But I keep trudging on, a spark from my bright torch shoots
And I hope that the small spark, ignites a different end
Then the feeling I am sensing, that's just around the bend

With time the rain and storms on our relationship did fall
It caused me to seek shelter, the wind did come to call
I did not abandon you, as I hid inside the cave
I needed to protect my light, its flicker I did save

And though we tried to continue, our destinies did vary
You needed to experience a new road and I was wary
I made my torch burn higher as you left and said goodbye
If the world would just burn brighter, no harm in shadows could then lie

As you ventured off, I continued on my way
My torch was growing heavy and my back did need to lay
So, I found a clearing up ahead, and a bonfire I did light
Its circumference was magnificent, it was quite a sight

I'll keep this large fire burning, in case you fall to harm
As you live your life on your own terms, and show the world your charm
And I'm hoping your roads fruitful, and you achieve your dream
But if you get lost, look up, for in the sky my fire will gleam

Family and friends, we are saddled with the chore of great success
To guide our kids and neighbors, so their lives won't be a mess
But all that we can do, is to be a good example
And keep a light well lit, that the world cannot trample

Following the Leader

Following-the-leader was a game we played when young
We trailed over, under, in a row, while the song was sung
There was only one lone leader and the rest of us would trail
There was no competition, no one who played could fail

As we moved into adulthood, the game we still are playing
We either don't admit it, or at least no one is saying
There are many leaders we now choose each day to align with
And what some say they stand for, with time proves to be a myth

There are leaders in our nation, healthcare, churches and our schools
We assume they all will follow what is best and moral rules
But have we blindly followed some bad people just the same
Are we naive as children, who once enjoyed the game?

It's time to pay attention to the ones who choose to lead
And evaluate intention, are they helping those in need?
And also note the followers who choose to never ask
The questions that need asking as they hide behind their mask

The world does need leaders and we can't all be the chosen
But evaluate them carefully, don't let your voice be frozen
Be proud to stand behind the ones you feel are right
And continue to love others even with their lack of sight

I do believe that light will always conquer over dark
The differences between the two in our world can be quite stark
Which is why the only leader that won't lead into temptation
Is the one that I am picking to help assist our struggling nation

This leader reigns above the rest and is always in the light
He helps makes sense of all the wrong, helps me follow what is right
I speak to Him daily and I feel His presence near
And if I keep my faith, I never have to fear

So the only one I trust, I can feel within my gut
And if I listen carefully, I will avoid the rut
God lives within my soul, the one I choose to lead
If we walk with Him in light, from the darkness we'll be freed

Car Rides with Dad

In February it began, the first ride that would be many
I was brought home from the hospital, the fare not even a penny
This began a blessed journey, I experienced with my dad
I thanked God quite often, for the father that I had

Our rides were oh-so-many, and became a treasured gift
I learned a thing or two about life when I needed a lift
We would listen to country music, talk over the day's event
I cherished our time together, a time that was well spent

He drove to dancing lessons, Sunday school or just to a friend's
Or to school if it was snowing, my wellbeing he always defends
As I grew I learned the value of conversations in the car
Silently prayed with my own children, the destination would be far

And as years did then progress, the driver we did change
Destinations now were the doctors, but our words we still did exchange
With me behind the wheel, I saw his life slipping away
No matter how I prayed, he couldn't forever stay

Conversations became deeper, we covered a lot of ground
I loved to hear his opinions, and he listened like no one around
I tried to calm his worries, his fears they were so grand
I asked him to say a prayer, that in God's arms they would land

On our final drive together, you had already left this earth
The ash that does remain, speaks nothing of your new birth
I played your country music, as a tear ran down my face
The love you left inside me, from my heart will never erase

Rest in Peace, Dad.

Downsizing

The day has finally come, as I watch the boxes go
Much thought to what was packed inside, my treasures all in tow
A few will come to my new place, and things I'll give away
And hopefully a small amount, in the family they will stay

I've outgrown this large place, no need for all the rooms
My days have become much simpler, my weeks are full of blooms
I'm grateful all the kids, in their lives are doing well
Our closeness not defined by the four walls, it's time to sell

I need less to maintain, and I've realized with time
The best things I've collected can't be purchased with a dime
And with my new found freedom, I will continue to add more
More love and life experiences, and fun are what's in store

There is a suitcase I have picked, I pack when I'm alone
It contains all of my treasures I've embraced as years have flown
I will be strong enough to carry this one suitcase, though it's large
It is light and not yet fully filled, and my soul it does recharge

As I arrive at my new home, I unpack each box with care
I've retained the special things that to my new space will add flare
But I won't unpack the items in the suitcase that I cherish
It's filled with all my memories that from my life will never perish

And I get to keep on adding to its contents each new day
All the love and memories I'll pack in will always stay
This very special suitcase is all I get to bring
When I make my final move back home, where my soul is free to sing

So worry not about the things we've collected here on Earth
They feel all important here, but up there they hold no worth
Instead experience all the things in life we've been given for free
The love we hold within our heart is what I am taking with me.

Do You Need Floss?

We've all been to a party, where we indulge in all the treats
We snack on dips and mingle, while we enjoy delicious sweets
We work our way around, the room in conversation
Get interrupted by a friend, who needs to share an observation

They quietly let us know, something's stuck between our teeth
We quickly use our hand, for cover as a sheath
We navigate our way, to the bathroom for a peek
We examine as we smile, what's underneath our cheek

Sometimes it's just a stain, and nothing's truly lodged
But sometimes it is a seed or some dill our swallow dodged
We're grateful for the friend, who pointed out what we can't see
Embarrassed isn't something, we want to feel or be

With this knowledge and assessment, we can then decide an action
Do we leave it as it's fine, or use floss for the extraction
There are things about ourselves, behavior, thinking or our ways
We may not always see; we may need others to appraise

And just like with our teeth, we take the comments to a mirror
A deep reflection in, will guide us where we want to steer
Is the way we think we are, always received as we intend
Or do we need to change some things, with the advice of a friend

Don't be angry at the friend, who wants what's best for you
I hope your life's complete with more than one or two
And for the friend who doesn't tell what they notice that you can't see
Ask yourself the question: in your life, should they be?

Favorite
Preferred Before All Others of the Same Kind

I struggle with the term favorite; it's involved when there's two or more
To me it involves competition, and I dislike it to my core
I do compete in life, but only with myself
To be better than I once was, is a book right off my shelf

When asked who is my favorite, I can honestly answer not one
I love each person uniquely, whether a daughter or a son
I liken it to a condiment, a silly example it's true
I choose mustard to eat with my ham, Al with my steak, how taboo!

And ketchup, my pork chop fave, though horseradish I sometimes select
With chicken I choose to use none, its flavor I don't try to perfect
Yet I doubt the condiments care, when I randomly choose what to use
Let's all try to be condiments, see the joy that each introduce

The thing is my heart has much room, to contain all of the souls that I love
It goes beyond my sons and my daughter, just like God shows us from above
I don't try to be His favorite, as He is an all-loving God
To compete for rank above others, is a principle I feel is flawed

There's really no need to compete when we see we're part of a whole
We all affect each other, and we each contain a soul
And when souls join all together, what magic they do produce
Love grows exponentially, and conflict does then reduce

Our hearts are quite expansive; they can stretch to quite a size
Let's focus on filling them up, competition can cloud our eyes
To all of you I love, know I love you in different ways
Thanks for being in my life; you brighten up my days

Goodbye Yellow Brick Road

My part was Dorothy. Was it just a grade school play or was it a foreshadowing of my life? Time would tell. As I think about this story, there are many significant parts to take note of.

We have all had cyclones in our life that throw our reality into orbit. I am no exception.

Thank God for all the Toto's who have shared my life and remained with me through good and hard times. We will meet again.

Thanks also to all the Glenda the good witches who guided me through life. There were more than a few. Your souls are pure love.

I am aware of the wicked witches who have tried to hinder my journey or placed obstacles in my path. And to the flying monkeys who helped them, I see you, too.

The munchkins remind me of the children in my life. They are completely dependent on others for their survival but are filled with joy.

And we've all experienced the poppies a time or two. We were disillusioned for a spell. It's good when we wake up from such things.

We've run into cowardly lions, who don't have the courage to do what is right. Scarecrows in life are all too common today; they don't have a brain to find truth. But the most difficult to travel with in life are the tin men who don't have a heart. We all know who these three beings are in our life. Forgive them for not being who you needed them to be and love them anyway. That doesn't mean you shouldn't have boundaries.

What do we find when we follow this yellow brick road and why is it yellow? Are we following a gold standard? Are there missing bricks? Is there significance to it leading to the Emerald City? It's odd the Emerald City is the same color as money. And that it led to an all-important wizard with all the answers…or did it? There is no wizard who has the power to get us home or save us. He was a fake behind a curtain. I often think of the things I have discovered in life by pulling back a curtain and finding a truth I didn't expect.

And the ruby slippers must represent my husband for whom I am so grateful. He supports me in all I do. He makes me feel pretty and sparkly. We are a perfect fit. And he follows me home.

To me, this play reveals that the power in life to get over the rainbow lies within me and not someone else. It has always been that way. I'm hoping you will come to the same conclusion when you visit the land of Oz.

Be Kind

In a world that's torn with chaos, on the nightly news we see
Violence, hate and anger, it's not what the world should be
How do we suppress it, a cure we need to find
It's solved with love and empathy, and the need to just be kind

Kindness means asking nicely, for the things we'd like to see
Saying *please* is easy, no rudeness needs to be
And *thank you* follows the gifts that we are freely given
Manners are what we should use, where our habits should all be driven

I'm sorry should also be used, when we misstep and hurt another
It's not always our intent, when we hurt a sister or brother
To recognize our behavior, to stop, look and reflect
Will give us a clue to our habits, and if others we respect

To teach our children these things, to make them grow up nice
Is something we need to model, not just tell them as our advice
They watch us more than listen, sometimes we are unaware
So, let's make kindness our lifestyle, and scatter it everywhere

Giving feels much easier, when we are just asked, *Please*
And *thank you* means they are grateful, for helping to put them at ease
A grateful heart brings more to us, abundance flows right in
There is so much to be grateful for, where do we begin

We often use *please* when we pray, and hopefully *I'm sorry*, too
Have we thanked Jesus enough, our life He does renew
He gave us all that He had, modeled how we should live
He taught us all the manners, and how to others to give

Let's give Him back the gift, by showing Him we have learned
The lessons He once taught, our eternity should be earned
Look to all His actions, and you will certainly find
He was the one who showed us, the value in being kind

Don't Judge a Book by Its Cover

I talked with an old man, and as his story did unfold
His appearance didn't match, the story that was told
It got me thinking deeper, about the way that we all judge
Do we really know another, is there reason for our grudge

We all have quite a story, no two are just the same
Each chapter holds a feeling: love, lessons, grace or shame
And we rarely read the whole book, on the people that we know
We believe their outer image, the cover that they show

Our stories contain chapters, some are pleasant and some are sad
Some make us feel joyful, some leave us feeling bad
The people in your life, might just have read a line or two
Can't understand your whole book, thought they knew you by review

And if you find yourself, in a hard part of your story
Turn the page, continue on, its ending can bring glory
You hold all the answers, to how your story will lay out
Try to pick a title worthy, so its content won't cause doubt

You may not like to read, as much as others do
Know that understanding, takes reading chapters, more than two
The one you thought you knew, you are likely to discover
The book that they have lived, should not be judged by their cover

Gone but not Forgotten

We think we have forever, then death knocks at our door
Our struggles are now over, the pain we feel no more
Our loved ones do then gather, memories felt within the heart
The good times are now treasured, from this world we do depart

The family binds together, support the broken husbands and wives
Picture boards that are assembled, reveal the fabric of our lives
And it's funny all we strove for, the stuff we did acquire
Didn't seem to make the cut, their value with us did expire

Our life reduced to pictures, and our children who carry the torch
The lessons all recalled, from our chats upon the porch
We hope they take the best parts, of who we tried to be
And forgive us for our errors, don't carry any debris

Our photos all contain people, showing times we spent together
The ones who stuck around, as life's storms we all did weather
The joy on all the faces, mark the quality of our bond
The love that is revealed, transcends this world and beyond

It's not the number of people, who in life we do impress
It's how many souls we do impact, how many we do bless
Our time on earth is short, make the most of it while you are here
The memories like waterfalls flow, as your loved ones shed a tear

And when the sun sets on my life, know I loved you with all of my heart
I'll remain right by your side, just my body I'll depart
Forgive me for hurts I have caused, know I valued our time together
Though I no longer walk on this earth, look for me I'll be wearing a feather

Chapter Three

Spirituality and Faith

This chapter presents faith as a source of strength and guidance. Poems like *Surrender* and *Answered Prayer* explore trusting divine timing, while *No God, No Peace; Know God, Know Peace* reveals the serenity found through connection with God.

Works like *Light Wins* and *The Heart of the Matter* illustrate faith's power to illuminate life's path, offering inspiring reminders of spiritual resilience.

Surrender

We are often called to surrender, but giving up is not how I roll
To me that negative thinking in life can take a toll
By pulling up my bootstraps, and not accepting defeat
I've succeeded at many things, and failure I did cheat

But then I got to thinking, is another view helpful to see
Can surrender ever be useful, where in it lies the key
Maybe it means don't resist that God does have a plan
Flow with all that happens, rest your worries in Him if you can

Stay out of your head and accept the things that get placed in your lane
They will work out for your best, when we live in our heart not our brain
It's important to stay at peace, as our life begins to unroll
Don't let worry and stress on your body take its toll

When we think of living this way, and surrender to what we are dealt
Rest assured that God will be present, His support will always be felt
I accept this type of surrender, and use it as my guide
I will not fight with my journey, and I'll keep my faith by my side

No God, No Peace
Know God, Know Peace

How many times we've heard, and we think we understand
Until life throws us a curve ball, it's not what we had planned
We repeat the phrase above, hoping pain will go away
But it doesn't always work, as in our brain our thoughts do stay

Knowing is a verb that takes place within our head
That also is the locale, of something we call dread
I believe it takes much more, than believing in a thought
There is another organ, that will help untie the knot

Our heart is where we feel, the peace that has been given
When united with our brain, it's a force that keeps us driven
To believe and have more faith, that rises over fear
If we think and feel the words, the message will be clear

And know this peace is given, to all who know the Lord
From a parent to a child, accepted not ignored
We never would return, a gift that is so grand
If we truly felt it's impact, we'd be calm and understand

So go ahead recite, and think about the phrase
But don't forget to feel it in your heart, your spirits raise
And be grateful for this gift that is often underused
It oozes love and hope, that to our life it will diffuse

Peace I leave with you: my peace I give to you;
Not as the world gives do I give to you. Let not your
hearts be troubled, neither let it be afraid (John 14:27 RSV).

Light Wins

Good wins over evil, darkness loses to the Light
When I tune into the news, it's hard to see that's right
So many things revealed, seem to be from the dark side
They look past all the goodness, and the truths they sure do hide

The people in my life, show me another side
I see smiles and kindness all around, and arms are open wide
To give a gentle hug, or help support you on your way
So many generous stories, exist throughout the day

The sun lights up the sky as we head out in early morning
The darkness comes at night and tries to issue us a warning
The dark does not prevail, as it's joined by a bright moon
Where it will light the sky, sunrise is coming soon

When two rooms are side by side, a closed door between them stands
One is filled with darkness, the other, where light lands
If you open up the door, that separates the two
Light falls into the dark room, and the shadows become few

The eclipse comes along, the two forces light and dark
Compete to rule the sky, The battle is quite stark
And for a moment darkness reigns, a peek at life without the light
Should help us with decisions, to fight for what is right

If you find yourself in turmoil, and can't seem to find the spark
Look up to find the light of God; He will lead us out of dark
And find comfort in this guidance as He lights the path we take
Good does win over evil, no matter the noise the dark make

For Such a Time as This

Demolition had to happen
The boards rotten to the core
It was overrun by rats
Its death at our front door

It once had served a purpose
Something died along the way
What it had become
Could no longer stay

So I sat and watched it happen
Every brick would be removed
The boards were hauled away
The dirt would all be smoothed

I dreamed about the new
A foundation to take its place
The support beams and safe harbor
On its way to the whole human race

So do not shed a tear
As you watch the structures fall
We've exciting things to come
Our requests to God quite tall

Please assist with the assembly
A helping hand gloved in new bliss
And be glad that you were born
For such a time as this

Truth

The quality or state of being true
That which is true or in accordance with fact or reality
A fact or belief that is accepted as true

What do we define as truth, is it different for you and me?
Does it change as we observe what we've been told and what we see?
Your parents love you more than any human ever could
Is this true for all the children, even when we think it should?

A child believes in Santa because that's what they've been told
By those who love them most, but life's truth will soon unfold
Respect those in authority, they always have your back
Are they really out for your own good or might compassion sometimes lack?

As we travel down this road, do our truths start to evolve?
Does the truth keep pushing out as illusions all dissolve?
Do these emerging truths help us open our ears, minds and eyes?
And might we change the way we think about things we once called lies?

As we question what is true, we explore what else could be
New things we learn may inspire you and may sometimes challenge me
Truth is a belief that is accepted at the time with what we know
But isn't life a journey on which our truths will change and grow?

Observe, question and keep learning and I think that you will find
Some amazing new truths and ideas if you keep an open mind
If we turn away and refuse to look and don't challenge our belief
We'll stay stuck in our old ways and our pains won't find relief

And if you learn a truth that's not popular in thought
Be grateful for the knowledge that to your life it brought
You don't need to stand on mountain tops or project it in a shout
The beauty in the truth is it will always find a way out!

The Heart of the Matter

We are given only one heart, that to our body does pump
But it has many facets, it isn't just a thump
A physical and a mental piece, are also held within
As well as the emotions, that are contained therein

The physical is easy, move your body to stay fit
With the mental, research foods to eat and the toxins you should omit
The emotional part is harder, but its impact can take a toll
Is the baggage coming from you, or someone else's to unroll

The pain in life can block us, if we leave it and don't address
It will fester and grow bigger, cause our life to be a mess
So, evaluate which facet of your heart causes an ache
Then look for the solutions, what new step is next to take

Above all else, guard your heart. For everything you do, flows from it
(Proverbs 4:23 NIV).

Answered Prayers

How often do we pray, for things we'd like to be
But when the answers given, we refuse to want to see
We accuse God of not listening, and not helping with our need
Truth is, He acts in many ways to help us to succeed

We may experience delays, to protect from what's ahead
Not included in the group, means not harmed by what is said
We might miss a flight or mate, or a promotion we desire
To reward us later on, with something that is higher

Perhaps things don't work out, as we need to learn a skill
Is it patience that is needed, live in peace, just be still
Trust the timing that He offers, but always stay alert
For when the signs are shown, to move forward and assert

Accept that all that happens, has a reason tied to it
Learn to see the meaning, or the lesson and submit
If we refuse to understand this, disease may then present
Bodies can give signs, for what is off, it's not pleasant

Or the bumps along the way, may increase in time and size
Are we seeing things objectively, or believing self-made lies
Life can be quite painful, but there's One who lights our way
He loves us unconditionally, so in the dark we will not stay

How do we turn the light on, so in the tunnel we will see
What He has laid before us, what He desires for us to be
Start you day in gratitude, for all the blessings in your life
Drop all of the worry, and the fears that cause you strife

Have faith things will work out, for your best as God has planned
The right people and right blessings, in your lap will surely land
And pray that God will give you, open eyes for you to see
The signs He lays before you, to be all that you can be

Let's Go Fishing

EGO…GOD…both three letter words
To think they've things in common, sounds quite absurd
But isn't it quite true, that they both have started wars?
How can this be, when they seem from separate shores?

Both containing the word GO, suggests action of some kind
EGO in service to self, not always healthy you will find
While GOD requests service, to others we might know
Our hearts are guided outward, where love is sure to show

If we are to swim in waters, and sail along in life
We need to find a balance, of the two to not cause strife
We can't reside on either shore, if we want to stay afloat
How much EGO, how much GOD, will you put inside your boat?

EGO is important, to maintain in small amounts
Taking care of self, makes us strong on all accounts
And with this new-found strength, we can then provide more aid
We might just be the answer, for something someone prayed

Evaluate your actions, and know from where their source
Do you need to make adjustments, to your sails on your course?
Or do you have the perfect balance, of EGO and of GOD?
If you do, I'd like to fish with you, if you have an extra rod

The Lord is My Shepherd, I Shall Not Want

There is comfort in being a sheep. Having someone to lead you to still waters and green pastures. Someone who provides you with a secure place to rest, safe from the wolves that hide in the darkness. Someone who makes all your decisions for you to free your mind up to just be.

Jesus came to be our Shepherd, to model how to live in Christ
He taught us all He knew. He spoke truth, faith and love.
There are other Shepherds this world offers to those who seek
to be sheep. They too will lead you somewhere. Be mindful
of where you are heading and who is leading you as there are also
wolves who exist. Many will dress as sheep.

I believe there is a lot to be learned if we listen to hear other's words. But there is more to be understood by observing their actions.

In these tumultuous times I ask myself, "What would Jesus do?"
His words tell me, "Follow Me."
And his actions tell me, "Be a Shepherd."

And I will give you shepherds after my own heart, who will feed you with knowledge and understanding (Jeremiah 3:15 NIV).

Chapter Four

Life's Challenges and Struggles

*F*ocusing on resilience, this chapter navigates adversity and strength in hardship. *Fear Not* and *Victim or Victor* encourage empowerment, while *Tug of War* reflects on societal divides. Poems like *Running Hurdles* and *The Fun House* use vivid metaphors to explore challenges and illusions. Together, these pieces inspire hope and determination to overcome life's struggles.

Fear Not

Why do we all fear? What do we have to gain?
When we let it in our thoughts, our mind will entertain
It causes great anxiety, and robs us of our joy
Yet we invite it in most days, our lives it does destroy

And do our worries and concerns ever come to be?
I think they don't as often as we expected we would see
But yet we choose to let it have a presence in our mind
I'm sure a better outcome in our life we can still find

How often do we read and actually hear what Jesus said
When He told us to "Fear not" for what may lie ahead?
In the Bible it was mentioned 365 times
So it shouldn't only happen on occasion or sometimes

We all claim to be good followers as we sit in church and pray
But how easily our thoughts and self-worth are led astray
It's easy to have faith, and fear not when life is good
But do you hold this peace when it's not going as it should?

So I challenge each and every one, in the midst of these great storms
To hold your peace and faith, until the world with love reforms
And know that God is walking by our side along the way
And the promise of "fear not" in our minds we should replay

Tug of War

Our lives were all quite busy, as we went about our day
When the world did suddenly halt, a game was required to play
No one was allowed exclusion, to stand by they did not permit
We all had to be in the match, our society truly did split

A rope was laid on the ground, the ends were fully in view
We were told to each choose a side, our choices side one or side two
A line was drawn down the middle, to cross it determined the win
To be pulled across by the other, would be the ultimate sin

The promises laid out before us, helped us pick which side to align
We did not understand that our choices, our identity now did define
Our families split to both sides, our friends did a similar thing
This game that we were now playing, didn't make my soul want to sing

For many aligned on the left, and fewer did stand on the right
The way it all sized up, it wasn't an even fight
Besides the uneven numbers, many things were yelled at the few
Their roles in life were in jeopardy, reputations were thrown out, too

The pulling began to happen, both sides they gave it their all
But it wasn't the side with the few who slowly began to fall
It seems that siding with many didn't offer a definite win
A number were dropping off quickly, and taking it right on the chin

With time the few were still standing, pulled the rest right over the line
The rope that held it together, diminished to nothing but twine
The victory was very hollow in this game we were forced to play
As we saw all those who had fallen, on the ground they would surely stay

They were our family and friends, that we lost as we held our ground
We heard their battle cries and regret as they muffled a sound
Why did we have to choose between our life and truth in our gut
To think that this was normal, you'd have to be a nut

So the question I honestly ask to those who understand
Why did we agree to play this game upon the sand
And who would ask our society, to partake in such a sport
Did they dislike us strong enough that our life they would extort?

The Fun House

I walked up to the Fun House, as my joy was more than lacking
No matter what I did, I felt sad, and my fun was slacking
I approached the older man, who held tickets to admit
Hoping to escape my life, and smile for just a bit

When I entered the main room, four doors stood shut before me
I entered the first one and floods of memories brought me glee
Then I saw some darker times, the good feelings didn't last
I realized I can't find joy by staying in the past

I tried another door, hoping this would turn out better
I saw the things I wanted, a new car and fancy sweater
I knew I didn't have what it would take to buy these things
Worrying about the future didn't help my soul to sing

The third door had to have the experience I was seeking
I was shocked to see folks in my life, each one of them was speaking
Some said such nice things, others didn't prove so kind
My sense of self felt wounded when I let them in my mind

I approached the final door with trepidation and some fear
A fun house without smiles, I might just shed a tear
The room behind this door, revealed each wall with a large mirror
I felt confused and left the room, my thoughts were not much clearer

I passed the older man at the ticket booth once more
I told him how confused I was, joy missing from each door
I didn't feel much better than when I first came in
He said I missed the meaning and would help to lift my chin

The last door that you opened helped you look at your reflection
You're the only one who matters, as you give yourself inspection
True happiness is found not in a past or future date
Not from other people, it's found within—it's not too late!

Running Hurdles

Remember running hurdles and we all loved to compete?
Bringing home a ribbon was a special kind of treat
We'd speed to reach the finish line, leaping as we'd go
Symbolic of our life, even though we didn't know

What if this kind of race was real life and not a game
Would it be set up differently, or would it be the same?
Some hurdles might look short, others seem to reach the sky
Some may be quite spaced out, others bunched for us to try

We may encounter most when young, or when nearly at life's end
To run them in the sun is nice, but rain the clouds could send
To run them during daylight, may work for some of you
Some may have to run at night, and it may be quite a few

And would we all compete, each in our own marked lane?
Or would it be a team sport, where we felt each other's pain?
You see we all run hurdles throughout life, it's not a choice
To encourage all your neighbors is a good use of our voice

And if we see them trip on a hurdle as they run
Let's help them back to standing, and not worry if we won
When it rains upon them, why not offer an umbrella
You might just realize that underneath, they're Cinderella

I wonder when we jump our hurdles early on
If we could just assist the rest instead of sitting on the lawn
To have a bit of compassion, as others complete their race
Would make the sport more peaceful, and the world a nicer place

And when someone is in the dark, why not offer them a light
There are times when life is difficult, and it doesn't feel quite right
To run hurdles in this way has a special kind of grace
And wouldn't life be better if we all finished the race?

The Marathon

The marathon had begun, the number who ran not a few
The hours of preparation, much more than one or two
All had the same destination, to reach the finish line
They departed the same location, their passions did align

But some had previous injuries, they healed before that day
They prayed their therapy remained worthy, that results would stay
They each ran for a different intention, some did it just for fun
Some accompanied another friend, daughter or a son

And people aligned on the route to offer some water or snack
So they could focus on running, there was nothing they would lack
Some were present at check points, others drove along the whole way
Some were there for a time, others remained to the end they would stay

On occasion, a runner would stumble, or be injured and cause them to drop
It may have affected this race, but others it would not let stop
They couldn't all possibly win, but to keep going and finish the course
Is where they showed their strength, perseverance was really a force

And isn't this much like life, in which we aim for a finish line
Where we can be so proud, how we lived, even on an incline?
There are people we run with, in this marathon we call life
There are some who push and shove, to our life they do bring strife

And who are those significant, ones who line your way
Are they present for the whole race, or for just a portion do they stay
Who offers you refreshments, as you face the glaring heat?
Who helps you in recovery? Who soaks and rubs your feet?

We should all hold understanding to those that stumble along
And feel at times this race is not where they belong
No one can know the injuries they carry on this road
We often lack the empathy, or we simply are not told

And no one will fully get what you went through to train
It wasn't just the physical, some things happened in your brain
So decide to run this marathon, and do it at your pace
Acknowledge those around you, but by all means, run your race

Lessons in the Mirror

When you look into the mirror, a reflection you will see
Do you like what then presents, as you say, "This is me"
Do you appreciate your features, and the body that you have
Or are you wishing to be different, seeking out a new best salve

Do you notice if you smile, a happy face does reflect back
And with a frown or worried look, your face will show the lack
And what do you suppose the difference is between
The one where joy exudes versus bad feelings that are seen

I believe it takes some action on our part to create both
We are the ones responsible, for our vision and our growth
For our gratitude and knowledge, what muscles to call forth
As the corners of our mouth, turn south or up toward north

And isn't this great mirror, very much like life itself
Will we use our gratitude to see, or place it on a shelf
Will we take the needed action, to create the life we want
Or allow all of the traumas forever to us haunt

If we understand it's up to us, to get the life desired
And yes it does take effort, and we sometimes may be tired
But the old familiar saying, we get back what we put out
Is absolutely true, of that I have no doubt

So when you look into the mirror, what do you really see?
Is there something that needs changing, to get to where you want to be?
Is there something that needs action, or do you just require new vision?
God gave you free will, it's always your decision.

Victim or Victor

In life we all face challenges, and our choice of response is two
We can be a victor, and our struggles will feel but a few
They look at life head-on, dig in and figure it out
Little time is spent crying, they are busy with a new route

And then there is the victim, who follows a different path
They complain and whine to others, in pity they take a bath
It is always somebodies fault, why they have a difficult time
It always happens *to* them, their voices repeatedly chime

I believe we're in charge of our thoughts, and our thoughts create our life
If we are happy we'll feel blessed; if not we'll be living in strife
We have a choice how we view things: do we take responsibility,
Or do we fold and give up, as we cry on bended knee?

The victor still has troubles, but his mind is a different kind
He fights to cut the chains, so he isn't stuck in a bind
And the victor knows who to ask, to solve the dilemma at hand
They look inside themselves, that's where their strength does land

While the victim requires another, someone who is at fault
They have no strength inside, from their high horse they do vault
To identify the perpetrator, the one who is to blame
Requires but a mirror, look who's inside the frame

My Ring of Keys

I step inside the building
Patterned tiles beneath my feet
The ring of keys I carry
Against my leg, they softly beat

Before me only doors
Nothing else this space does hold
Each one looks quite unique
My choices many, so I'm told

Each key unlocks but one
I've no time to choose them all
As I shuffle through the ring
I wonder where my choice will fall

As I open up the doors
That match selected keys
My reactions vary greatly
Peace and love to bended knees

In life these keys and doors
Are the thoughts we daily choose
Different outcomes with each threshold
Will cause us to win or lose

And why do we believe
When rooms are dark, no light we find
We can't turn around and run
Back to the hallways of our mind

You hold all the keys
God gave you all free will
If your thoughts hold all the answers
Will you stay in darkness still?

Why Do We Assume?

In life we make assumptions on things we think are true
They are based upon a feeling and the facts are usually few
We let them sway our thoughts and commit them to belief
Where they can do more damage and not provide relief

Most things I see that we assume are of a certain kind
They usually believe the worst, no hope that they can find
We aren't qualified for the position that we'd like
Or the one who holds my heart, may tell me to take a hike

Our offer on the house, they never will accept
My friends won't have my back, and my secrets won't be kept
My family thinks I'm still a kid and won't be proud of me
I'll never measure up, my success will never be

I don't have all the qualities, to hang with this type of tribe
I am not of the same caliber, their opinion I can't describe
They never will appreciate the gift that I picked out
They never will believe me, even if I stand and shout

And the luck that others have, when we say the same old prayer
Is because we are not worthy, to think better we don't dare
You see all these assumptions we've concocted in our mind
They really are projections we put out for life to find

But what if our assumptions were more positive than dark?
Our life would follow suit, and new results would start to spark
We've been told that to assume makes an ass of you and me
So take care of all your thoughts, and your destiny you will free

Expectation

What is an expectation?
How does it come to be?
Are we looking through the proper lens
For what we hope to see?

A job that has no stress
Promotions and pay that are fair
To get along with all at work
Vision and morals we share

The spouse that has no flaws
Their salary fills our life up
To be an equal parent
And to always fill our cup

The group of friends we're close to
That will always have our back
To have fun and never be challenged
And we run in a large pack

The family and parents who raise us
Unconditional love we reap
Alike in every way
And no one is a black sheep

Our bodies that we live in
That house our very soul
Every part looks perfect
And our lifestyle takes no toll

Our groups that we belong to
All share a common goal
Who accept us without question
No one's in control

Are expectations possible
To be met in every way?
Or is our thinking fantasy
That society creates each day?

I do believe in dreaming
Goals and visions I'd like to see
But it's wrong to have expectations
On how they will come to be

There is no perfect scenario
That idea creates sadness and blame
Life has many great choices
Not one that we all aim

Who is the one to decide
What's best for you and me?
Is there a perfect answer?
I think not; let your life be free

So, consider your expectations
Are they real or too good to be true?
Do they set you up for low self-esteem
And keep your thoughts and life blue?

You don't know anyone well enough
To assess what you don't have and they do
Stop comparing yourself to others
And to yourself be true

Life doesn't check all of the boxes
But not everything is bad
Gratitude for what we do have
Is what prevents us from being sad

If you have worry and fear
And your life feels like a wreck
Take a moment to think
Are my expectations in check?

Chapter Five

Self-Reflection and Inner Peace

This chapter invites readers to introspect and reconnect with their inner world. *Come Upstairs* and *Wake Up* inspires rising above fears. At the same time, *Stained Glass* encourages unity amidst divisions, and *The Grass is Always Greener* rejects comparison in favor of gratitude. The poems serve as tools for finding peace and authenticity within.

Come Upstairs

I'm surrounded by collections of old things. Dust fills the air.
I hear, *Come upstairs.*

I feel the cold and dampness where I stand
I hear, *Come upstairs.*

The darkness engulfs me as my candle begins to flicker
I hear, *Come upstairs.*

Loneliness creeps through my pores as I feel separated from the
laughter above
I hear, *Come upstairs.*

Whether it is from the basement of our home
Or the basement of our heart and minds,
We need to rise up.

Rise up and leave what we have collected from our past.
Rise up to feel the warmth and see the light.
Rise up to join the laughter.

You may need to take one step at a time
But by all means, come upstairs.

Seek and You Will Find

Sometimes we find ourselves on streets of great despair
Where can we find solace? Where do people care?
There are many houses on this street, which one will guide us out?
Which will bring the water, take us out of this great drought?

It is best to keep on walking past houses that are called
Power, fame or money won't lead to rainbows, they'll be stalled
Look to the house of hope, the one that's labeled *Love*
It has the key to peace, you will fly just like the dove

As you enter this abode, pay attention where you turn
There are hallways to the left and right, some of them will burn
To turn down to the left, two doors will then present
Labeled *Church* and *Family*, they are sure to be pleasant

As you enter do take note, are there conditions to be met
Before love is feely given, we may notice and regret
It's okay to feel the sadness, but do turn around in time
There's another hall to walk down, and its doors are more sublime

The hallway to the right, has three doors that can be seen
God, *Children* and *Pets*, my heart feels full, and love feels clean
You see this is the hallway of unconditional love
Their actions are just pure, no conditions like above

And yes, there are some doors, in this hallway like the left
That can give you this same feeling, but if whole there is a cleft
I'm confident you've noticed other doors in this great home
Where do they reside, as the halls you freely roam?

Pay attention to the ones who misuse the name of God
Look beyond the words, to see the real facade
And protection to the children, and animals they may hurt
A shield of love surround them, all pain it will avert

Even in the house of love, there are those that will deceive
Look within your heart and gut, God's guidance you'll receive
And bless those in your life, giving unconditional love
Know that they are sent from the Father up above

Shhh...

The thing with dirty secrets, is they're never secrets long
The truth always comes out, usually not harmonious song
Words cannot be changed, or forgotten once they're spoken
The wounds they leave are deep, and relationships get broken

If a thought you have is not spoken directly to the one
With whom you have concern with, the talk should not be done.
And if you can't convey, what you think in a nice way,
I hope they aren't spoken—in your mind I hope they stay.

For all the words we speak, should bathe in love and light
We should lift each other up, not chop down or start a fight
And if our truths do differ, as in life they sometimes will
Respect the other person, it's their journey to fulfill

My hope is all the people that I've let into my heart
Can be their authentic selves, or I fear we'll need to part
Don't feel the need to smile, and act kind when we're together
Then talk behind my back, those storms we will not weather

If I have contributed to conflict in any way
Know that I am sorry, in the past it will all stay
For life is all too short, to continue down that path
I want your full potential, not a life that's filled with wrath

God bless you on your journey, as I know He does with mine
I've forgiveness for all actions, that in the darkness do not shine
I want my inner circle, filled with love and so much more
If you cannot exist there, I wish you peace and there's the door

What Do You Do in Your Kitchen?

To all the bakers in our life, we praise you for your treats
It brings a bit of joy, to the food that each one eats
A mix of sugar and flour are the foundation for what they make
Then they add in other things, and in the oven it does bake

It requires one to follow the recipe at hand
To vary from it isn't wise, discipline it does demand
To alter the amounts, or ingredients within
Will most likely cause a failure, but you'll probably stay thin

But cooking is a different beast, it allows us to explore
The recipes are just a guide, we can add what we adore
It brings out creativity, and our gifts can be revealed
In the foods that we create, what our table now does yield

In life are you a baker, or would you say you're a cook?
Do you want the exact directions, listed out in a nice little book
And would it limit all the things, you could become in life
Whose recipe would you follow? Would it keep you free of strife?

Or are you willing to pursue, your time here with just a guide
To explore all of your options, no end result to which it's tied
What could you create, that would be a tastier dish
To add or subtract content, to adjust as you would wish

It's not an either-or, that we must all decide
But evaluate your time on each, and how it should divide
Every now and then, the bakery can be fun
But spending your time cooking, yields results that surely stun

Stained Glass

Division is defined as separation into parts
I believe that's where a downfall in our history often starts
To pit us against our neighbor, is part of the grand plan
To destroy the world we know, it's where it all began

So are we more divided, as we take a look around
I believe we are on many fronts, our situations quite profound
The color of our skin, our age, what sex we are
Our religion, politics, medical choices cause a scar

I wonder who it benefits for us to break apart
Is there an evil intent there, or is it from the heart?
Last time I checked we all are One Nation Under God
We are called Americans, but our reputation's flawed

Our differences are what made this nation oh so great
We are a melting pot of souls, together is our fate
So, lets pick up the pieces of our lives like shattered glass
And create a great mosaic. Though it's stained, its full of class

And let's stop the division and look how far we've come
If you feel the wrong direction, lets join forces, become one
For divided we will fall, united we will stand
We need to come together under God, let love expand

A zipper cannot zip without the other side
A clap no sound it makes, if one hand is tightly tied
But when we all join hands and unite all back together
Americans are strong, and any storm we'll always weather

Wake Up

I closed down my computer, finished up for the day
Twelve hours was enough, I didn't want to stay
The office was quiet, no one here but me
I would head to the door, at last I'd be free

The hallways were dark, the shadows were scary
I saw movement ahead and I became wary
The figures moved quickly, and the masks that they wore
We're not who they portrayed; I didn't know what was in store

I reached for the door to escape my uneasy
Found it locked up tight, my stomach felt queasy
My mouth was a desert as I drank from the fountain
I think I drank poison, my problems were a mountain

I felt something grab at my leg and I jumped!
Feeling faint and lightheaded, the blood from my heart pumped
Then I realized what was happening as my wife brushed my leg
"Time to rise and shine. Off to work! Want an egg?"

I sat up in the bed, wiped the sweat from my brow
No more awful thoughts to this day I'd allow
As I sat on the side of my bed in reflection
I wondered the link to my life, the connection

Did I feel in a trap as I went through my day?
Did I make enough time for fun, love and play?
Were the prominent people in my life that I brought
Really good to the core, like I had once thought

Was the water and food that sustained me the best
Or was my ingestion just some kind of a test
Were the hours that I worked productive and fair
Or were they too many, from my balance they'd tear

And was all the darkness I saw in my dream
Over emphasized in my mind and not what it seemed
My life is not bad as this dream made it feel
If I could wake up to what is most real

We live all our lives stuck in quite a story
And many a day, that robs us of glory
Don't be afraid to step out from the scene
And live a life, a script not yet foreseen

Telephone

Who doesn't love a campfire, and how it makes you feel
It melts away our worries, and brings joy this world can steal
And to add to its enjoyment, we often play the game
of *Telephone*, we see if the message stays the same

We join in a large circle, and a phrase whispered to one
continues round the circle, where the words become undone
By the time it reaches back, to the one who was the start
We laugh at how the phrase has changed, its meaning did depart

The game brought such great fun, as we laughed at what we heard
What the last person said, was really quite absurd
But was there meant to be, something more to this fun game
Were we to learn a lesson, for in life it is the same

To hear a spoken word, from some other than the source
Involves another's ears, and understanding, so of course
the message will start changing, when we hear things from another
It doesn't matter who, whether a sister or a brother

And the longer the chain is, the more distorted it becomes
We need to use discernment, from our gut is where it comes
We need to ask the question: *Did I witness what was said?*
Or am I just believing a distortion I've been fed?

Technology makes this process a bit harder to discern
Is the person and the message even real, is my concern
God gave us many senses, to evaluate what we feel
So use them to determine, what is fake and what is real

Right now we're living in, a time of great confusion
And many things presented, are nothing but illusion
Maintain your sense of humor as you watch this game play out
And remember *Telephone*, and what its lesson is about

The Grass is Always Greener

How often we compare with everyone around
We want to be like them, or have their blessings that abound
But is it mere perspective, on what is truly best?
Do they feel the same, as their life they do digest?

As I walk around in life, I observe so many things
A single person wants a mate, while married ones, divorce gives wings
The unknown desire fame, famous crave some privacy
The young want to be older, elderly from age they flee

The poor seek to be rich, thinking all will then be fine
Wealthy desire the peace, lost in the process as they shine
The desire to look like others, as we use unnatural ways
One more child to be like them, may not be where your story lays

For one, we are not meant, to strive to be the same
No great civilization, from this thinking ever came
And also, it encourages us, to seek joy from the outside
When we should look within, society has often lied

Embrace who you are now, shoot an arrow for your dream
Not based on other people, but what's inside to make you beam
No one has it all, we truly each have just enough
To climb to where we should, even when the trail feels rough

So water your own grass, stop looking at your neighbor's yard
We all can create beauty, even when the dirt is hard
Find the fertilizer, that helps you gain success
Aim for thick green grass, my hope for you is nothing less

Triggers

We all have triggers in our life, things that can make us upset
The car that cuts you off, someone smoking a cigarette
Or the friend who always shows up late, or the one who never comes
Or maybe it's loud noises that are made from neighbor's drums

Or is it something simple like when cabinets don't get shut
The toothpaste left inside the sink, the grass that didn't get cut
Perhaps the way that someone talks, or the tattoos that they now wear
Is it other's personalities or their traits that make you swear

How do we handle triggers, when things get underneath our skin
Do we turn to alcohol or drugs, do we curse and feel anger within
Do we try to eat our way on out, of the feeling that's inside
Do we choose to exercise too much or get in a car and ride

Or do we keep it bottled up and hide it from the world
Not to be addressed, no meaning to be unfurled
Where it can cause us anguish, and rob us of our joy
And be just like a splinter, our lives they do destroy

We'd be better to uncover, just why they irk us so
Why it bothers us so badly, we really need to know
So we can heal the parts of us, that are wounded and not well
And get rid of the unrest in life, the memories we'd expel

Look inside your triggers, get to know just why they're there
Your joy in life will thank you, and with others you should share
So they can understand, just how to heal themselves
And not store up their upsets or stack them on the shelves

The more we understand our triggers we can heal
The traumas hidden in our minds, we truly can reveal
And if we choose to never question what's going on inside
We may just pull the trigger on our life, our joy denied

Image:
The General Impression a Person Presents to the Public

What affects our image, many things do come to mind
Our truth and character of course, and honesty well defined
And then there is the physical, the package that carries it all
Society places much weight there; its demands can feel quite tall

And to which voices are we listening, to develop the image desired
Do they guide us to our true self, allow our voice to speak as required?
Or do we often fall victim, to the criteria and demands of another
To fit in often forces suppression, authenticity buried will smother

When we think about our physical, in the mirror we see our reflection
Do we judge our looks through the world, or see our image with utmost affection
If we look beyond the physical, we can see within the soul
The traits that are most important, set by God as our main goal

So check yourself and your thinking, what is most important to you
As you develop your image, and share it with more than a few
Are the things that you desire, mainly in physical form
Does this hold more weight than some others, do priorities need to reform

Live intentionally every moment, create the image with which you align
The only opinions that matter, are yourself and the divine
Step out in the world with confidence, no attention to what others think
If you're honoring what is most precious, let their harsh words and opinions all sink

As long as we desire, an image that serves our God
And don't fall for society's illusions, they often are a façade,
We will create an authentic image, one that we can be proud
To shine into the world, an example, let others be wowed

Where is Your Focus?

Have you ever watched karate? It's more than just a sport
It teaches discipline, the lessons in life will support
Practice well your craft, until victory you achieve
It's a lot about the mind, and what you do believe

To watch the kids line up, to break through the wooden block
The anticipation builds; to break it for some would shock
Some do not have a problem, as they swing their hand on through
Some will need to keep trying, their technique they need to review

The blocks are equal in size; they are held exactly the same
If they don't achieve their goal, it's their vision that's really to blame
You see they need a focus, on the other side of the board
To push their hand right through it, just like it was a sword

To think about the wood, will always stop the hand
On the top side of the board, is where the try will land
And isn't this like life? Our obstacles are the board
When we focus on solutions, we will see a big reward

And the face on the ones in class, who accomplished the difficult task
Glowed with a can-do look, in their glory they did bask
To accomplish a goal this big, by changing the focus locale
Surely does increase, self-esteem and their morale

So in life, try not to focus on the obstacle in your path
Look beyond the solutions, envision a good aftermath
This simple, small technique, will help you achieve success
Practice does make perfect; yourself you may just impress!

Opinions Matter

We all have our opinions, that's how society grows
We exchange them with each other, and solutions from them flows
But where do they come from? Are they always based on truth?
We may need to sometimes question the lessons from our youth.

Our opinions often form, from what happened as we grew
The good, the bad, the lessons, challenge all we ever knew
Since we each are so different, and our experiences often vary
Uniting our opinions can be helpful, not so scary

But on a different note, judgement is involved
It may hinder all our progress, the way forward can't be solved
And judgement often happens, not by what we see or hear
But what we're told by others, often linked out of fear

Judgement can be good, like when we judge a situation
Is it safe for us to enter, our gut gives information
Is the contract one we want, after what we've seen in past
Did we learn something from what happened? Did our lessons last?

My belief is my opinions should evolve with space and time
As I learn more information, I may change my paradigm
And my judgements should be based what I feel within my soul
Not use them about others, misunderstandings take a toll

"Judge not lest you be judged," should stay anchored in our mind
A better guide in life, I doubt you'll truly find
So let's welcome the opinions, and not judge the one who gave
Move forward from your heart, and society you might save

The Gift

As Christmas season rolls around, emotions fill the air
Preparations do begin, and our company we share
Each year I feel the joy, as we're all excited to give
But there's a heaviness that exists, I can't shake and can't outlive

I feel it as I'm shopping, the sadness for those who do struggle
Who can't afford the best present, as finances they do juggle
And what about some others, no family remains to enjoy
Or are they just not near, as their unit will soon deploy

I dislike the focus on gifting, on this holiday every season
And yet I contribute like others, not sure how to change it with reason
I know the wisemen gave gifts, it's most likely how once it did start
We've lost sight of the meaning of Christmas, the gifts meant to be a small part

It's to celebrate the arrival, of Jesus who came down to earth
He's the promise for our future, granted us from the moment of birth
As I thought on this more deeply, other birthdays we celebrate
We only buy gifts for whose birthday, falls upon that date

When did we start buying, for everyone on this day
Instead of giving to Jesus, the one to whom we pray
What would he most want, for his birthday we celebrate
I think I have an idea, let's wake up before it's too late

He wants us all to succeed, and be kind and full of love
To be filled with joy and peace, represented by the white dove
He gave us all the tools, and taught us how to achieve
To use all our God given gifts, is what he'd want I believe

To treat living things with respect, no judgement within our heart
He'd want us to guide and help others, we all could do our part
This I believe is the gift, we would all be wise to give
It's the greatest thing to give back, for the promise we now live

Make giving a regular thing, not just once throughout the year
As others fall in need, the present will seem quite clear
As you celebrate this Christmas, your focus you'll need to discern
Give a gift back to Jesus, it's the one gift no one will return

Chapter Six

Parenting and Generational Ties

This chapter highlights the nurturing bonds between generations. Poems like *Be an Eagle* offer wisdom on guiding children, while *Batter Up* reflects on parenting's dual roles.

Oak Tree celebrates familial roots, and tributes like *Raise Your Glass to Strong Women* honor resilience across generations. These works cherish the ongoing impact of parental love.

Be an Eagle

Aim to be an eagle, to fly higher than the rest
It is a good position, in which to build our nest
A bigger picture it will show, as we view life from above
It will help us find the meaning, and with our whole heart love

As we raise our little eaglets, we will teach them all we know
Things that will be needed for the world they see below
We will teach them how to love, themselves also a must
We will teach them what to eat, so they don't wither into dust

To forgive and to apologize are also needed things
To live a life of joy, and find the happiness that it brings
Appreciation for the gifts, to our life as they are given
To find purpose and the energy from which we all are driven

And as our little eaglets from the nest are then escorted
They will need to find their wings, the first flight feels unsupported
We can fly right by their side, but it's on them to take new flight
Eventually they'll be on their own; we will be out of sight

And as the crows in life present, either people or flying debris
We hope they watched how to adjust, by rising to a higher degree
For at that elevation, the crows will fall away
It's not worth entertaining the fight, and in our lives they surely won't stay

To be an eagle requires a risk as we take the very first jump
And leave our nest of security, as our wings they start to pump
To stay stuck inside the nest is a life that is wasted and sad
But when we soar as we are intended, that can never be bad

Batter Up

He had just retired, hung up his cleats and glove
He felt mighty blessed, his work was the game he loved
He hit many a strike, had some breaks and bruises, too
And never got the call from some teams, which made him blue

He watched all of the pros, and he coached with some great guys
He didn't miss a practice, and his dream did start to rise
He had determination, his work ethic served him well
He became a mighty player, his old self was but a shell

He couldn't fully walk away from the love for this great game
He couldn't hang it up yet, after winning Hall of Fame
So he decided to try coaching and help out a boy or two
Achieve the dreams they had; he'd teach them all he knew

He had to admit it, he had some favorite kids
Pete and Charlie were just that, but special treatment he forbids
Pete was just like coach, when he was a young man
And Charlie was the type of whom each teammate was a fan

A successful season played, and the coach was more than tough
His passion and his tips, could at times sound a bit rough
And when they'd finished playing, and the last out had been called
He met with each young teammate, the highs and lows were then recalled

Charlie knew few men like the coach to help him grow
He thanked him for his guidance, and the lessons he did show
While Pete did thank him too, but had some new ideas to try
The coach knew he'd succeed, and his hits would surely fly

He wanted to advise, as their careers did move along
Charlie was all for it, but Pete sang a different song
He asked if he'd stop coaching him, his help 'til then made him glad
But he wanted Coach to watch him play, and just be plain old Dad

Coach walked past the dugout, on his way back home than night
The grin upon his face, it really was a sight
You see in his career; he hit it out the park
But the ins and outs of parenting, sometimes left him in the dark

The moral of the story: in one area we may shine
But we will always keep on learning, to make all parts of life fine
Sometimes the way to help the children we do love
Is let them watch our game, from the bleachers just above

Give Thanks

Thanksgiving is a special time to reflect on all our blessings
We enjoy a meal with others, full of turkey, potatoes, and dressings
When we focus on all that we have, we see the world that surrounds
There are many ways to help others, examples do abound

But it frustrates me quite often when I do make a donation
The increased mailings I receive, my gift has devaluation
The costs to send them out have diminished what I gave
I don't feel like I have helped; the impact was just waived

No appreciation for the gift, which was easily received
I lost my faith in them, changed what I had once believed
There are so many places we can give and aid another
Choose them wisely as you seek, let your blessings on them smother

I thought a little deeper, does God sometimes feel the same
No appreciation for our gifts, our lack on him we blame
Is he likely to give more, with no gratitude in our hearts
For the blessings we do have, and the struggles he departs

So on this holiday, let us reflect on all the good
Appreciate each given gift, as we expect that others should
This opens up your life to more blessings from above
Be sure to share them all, as it's all about the love

Here's to Strong Women

Here's to strong women I knew as I grew:
There was Fannie, Aggie, Judy and Lou
And many more I observed on the way
I watched and I listened to all they would say

I noticed their struggles and how they survived
I saw what they did and how they revived
I witnessed their gratitude for all that they had
And how they found hope when at times they were sad

I observed all the work they put into their day
And as the sun set, to their God they would pray
I loved all the times we would talk and find joy
It ignited my spirit and my drive did deploy

There was no competition they felt with each other;
We are blessed in this life to have more than one "mother"
To encourage another is never a threat
There are many goals we have each in our lives set

And the men in their lives, not seen as inferior
Neither men or women to God are superior
They functioned together, each side of a team
And accomplished a lot, their marriage did beam

Find the strong women in this world where you live
To the ones that are not, we let go and forgive
And give back in return to the ones that we've chosen
And raise up your daughters in the love that this grows in

Now raise your glass and let's offer a toast
The great women above would not ever boast
They deserve my thanks for all the great lessons
I value them more than all my possessions

My message to all if we are to succeed:
Know them, be them, raise them, indeed!

Patterns

I've listened to the world and the things that I've been told
By those who are quite close to me, the truths now do unfold
My nationality isn't what I thought, it proved not true
There are things within our history, that can make all of us quite blue

You see we do become what those close to us do think
And if we grab ahold of that, our souls may start to sink
We need to stop the listening, and look out from our own eyes
To observe what is the truth, and what may be someone's lies

I've learned to see the patterns in the world as I do view
There are many that exist, and many are not new
The weather varies daily, it holds patterns just the same
The seasons come and go, and the winds will always tame

I see patterns in our nature, spider webs and honeycomb
Constellations overhead, that light up above our home
And history repeats itself, if its lessons we don't learn
By seeing all the patterns, find the ones that need to burn

The greatest pattern to observe lies in our family tree
What do we truly love, what do we *not* want to see?
Are we creating new or living what's been done before?
If we watch all the past patterns, we should know what is in store

And if it's not the direction that leads your heart and soul
We need to set some boundaries, live our life in a new role
For love and joy God did intend, for us to fully live
He gave us eyes to see, where our energy we should give

Look deep within the mirror, what was planted as a seed?
Do the patterns you have learned lead to success or will you bleed?
Do you see the cracks reveal, the truths we try to hide
It's not too late to change, the you that is inside

What a blessing we would bring, to others in the world
If we changed some broken patterns and our love is now unfurled
Would our children thrive and grow, in this new web that we could weave?
If we simply saw the patterns that from our lives should truly leave

Now embrace all the good patterns, that your family to you did give
And discard the broken shards that can make life so hard to live
And know we have a compass to guide us as we look
Jesus was an example and He left to us a great Book

The Power of Words

A child points towards a toy or book on a shelf,
or the bowl of food desiring more
Parents say, "Tell us what you want," or, "Use your words."

A toddler is upset and melts down
No skills yet to deal with the emotions they feel
Parents say, "Tell us how you feel," or, "Use your words."

A student feels frustrated and dumb
An assignment they don't understand
Parents say, "Ask the teacher," or, "Use your words"

An adolescent feels adoration for another
Too shy to let them know
Friends say, "Ask them out," or, "Use your words."

A young adult works so hard to get ahead
The promotion always goes to another
Others say, "Ask for the raise and position," or, "Use your words."

We have been raised to use our words for what we want or need
at every phase of life. But what if our words would be better spoken
for what others need instead of what we want?

The spouse who spends more time looking at the few faults of their soulmate instead of letting them know all the things they love about them

The parent who assumes the child knows how much they are loved
But the words are never spoken when the child needs to hear it most

The employee who never hears that the owner recognizes and appreciates their work

The apology that needs to be said for others but our egos get in the way

The forgiveness that needs to be given but wounds are too raw to do it

You see, some things in life are not meant to be asked for. Our words when spoken for others' sake carry the most weight and the greatest rewards.

So go forth with love, and use your words the way God intended them to be used

Chapter Seven

Nature as Teacher

Through nature's wisdom, this chapter draws parallels to human growth. *Cross the Stream* and *Climb Your Mountains* use challenges in nature to reflect resilience, while *The Gift of the Horse* teaches simplicity and equality. From appreciating unique paths to finding strength in nature's cycles, the poems inspire readers to look to the natural world for guidance.

Cross the Stream

As I walk along the riverbank, I take in all the views
I love to feel the earth beneath, as I carry both my shoes
I see I'm on the shaded side, and I look across the stream
The sun lights up the flowers, and the scenery is a dream

To cross this body of water is what I need to do
To smell the vegetation, hear the birds and see their hues
But how to go about it as the river rages on
As I ponder on my tactic, I look up to see a fawn

It looks into my eyes, its thoughts flood through my mind
The clear message overtakes me, more direct I'll never find
I need to use the boulders that are placed in front of me
To conquer all my fears, from the shadows I'll be free

The rocks are placed strategically, and they vary much in size
They represent my traumas and my fears, choices have ties
As I step upon the first one, the fears come flooding in
I focus on the journey as my courage can run thin

Some steps are easier to overcome, some others quite a climb
Slow and steady move along, I need to take my time
I hold my focus only on the next one in my path
Or my thoughts will overtake me and deliver quite a wrath

I am filled with joy and awe as I reach the side full of sun
And my senses overwhelm me with traumas I've overcome
To cross was more than difficult, yet it was worth the bruises and bumps
The confidence and knowledge from the fawn, my soul it jumps

We all have boulders in our lives we can use to see the light
If we choose the opportunities and dig in for just that fight
To reach the other side, where all the beauty lays
Is what we all desire and for each night we surely pray

So take your foot off the safety that resides on banks of shade
Be courageous in the journey, and your dreams won't ever fade
When you face the fear that so often comes on in
Remember the young fawn, and its message from within

The Gift of the Horse

The path along the lake was as serene as it could be
Void of all the pressures life gives us to not feel free
The breeze is gently blowing, the birds I can hear sing
The water looks like glass and reflections it does bring

As I look far to my right, a majestic horse is coming my way
It's very look and presence, I'm aware I'll want to stay
It beams with inner beauty, its white color pure as snow
Its aura shines pure love and light, and peace throughout it flows

Between us lies two creatures to its left and to its right
The horse cannot yet see them and inside I feel a fright
For to the right lies in the grass, a sheep underneath the trees
But to the left a lion waits to pounce on what it sees

The beautiful white creature veers left as it draws near
The direction it has chosen will end sad I truly fear
I'm joyfully amazed the lion allows it to pass by
And the lion holds its focus on the sheep; I wonder why…

As the horse comes to my side and I look into its eyes
I understand completely, its not bound to earthly ties
Its vision has been different since it was just a foal
God has given it a gift, and it can only see the soul

It's unable to see the package that our soul is neatly dressed
It's unable to hear the labels that society has impressed
It can tell if living things are pure or have dark intent
Not by what they're dressed in or identities they may rent

Confused, I change my focus back to the lion and the sheep
I see the sheep discard its coat, the wolf's identity it did keep
And inside the strong proud lion, a king at its very core
I see a great protector from the sheep and what was in store

And as I stand beside this great creature by the lake
I look into the water and the reflection that we make
It borrowed me its vision, and I can clearly see
The light and love inside me and from my labels I am free

How great and easy life would be if our differences we could shed
And judge others only by the light that's inside, their intent so easily read
It would help us to veer left, and not fall prey to darker beings
And guide us to the pure of heart who might share our similar feelings

We could toss out our meaningless labels that take over our busy world
Sex, race, religion, size, age, or profession in the bushes could all be hurled
And people would feel no shame about not fitting societies mold
And need only be concerned with the amount of light their soul does hold

Imagine the hurt and the judgments that would no longer have a place
To look deep within a person, our opinions on them we would base
So walk with the majestic white horse as you head out on your day
Try to lose all the judgments, pray its vision in your eyes will stay

Climb Your Mountains

Have you ever climbed a mountain? If so, why did you climb?
To see the other side, you could walk around it in less time
Maybe it's the option of taking in a better view
Maybe it's the challenge that creates a better you

The climb requires a couple things, to accomplish this great task
The mindset to hold focus on what's up, in the sun you'll bask
Some water and a check cord will be needed as you go
And one who climbs beside you, to celebrate on the plateau

You will need to reach up high, to get to next elevation
You will need to check your footing, focus on your respiration
Moving up requires you leave a spot that feels secure
To get to the next level, on this mountain you procure

It feels like this is life, we all have mountains that present
Do you take on the challenge, or walk around and just resent
Do you keep looking up, your path is not back down
It takes a lot of work, that's how your dreams won't drown

Do you understand that rising, requires comfort to be lost
Staying firm in your old footing, will surely have a cost
And who acts like your check cord, who always has your back
And who climbs by your side, who helps carry your backpack

I hope you climb your mountains, and reach the very top
The journey makes you grow, and its benefits don't stop
For help and sincere thanks, to above I hope you pray
The view that you'll take in, will take your breath away

Oak Tree

There was an oak tree on a hill, its roots were broad, its branches filled
With leaves all colors to behold, the acorns dropped before the cold
Its bark was worn and weathered, scars of storms that didn't last
Its girth held all the knowledge, rings of generations past
As clumps of acorns fell, they were planted in the earth
And with the spring and sun, a new family tree did birth
As seeds of the old oak tree broke away but didn't leave
Our roots remain connected, in this forest that we weave

What's in Your Garden?

Life is like a garden
We each create our own
What does yours have in it
Is the path of brick or stone?

Are there flowers bright and colorful
Are there different shades of green
Does your garden reflect all of you
And everything you mean?

Is it a work in progress
Daily tending required to bless
Or is it a one-time planting
That you let fate decide success?

Do you share your plants with others
How do your garden friends rate
Do they help add to your garden
Or should they be ushered to the gate?

Are there spots left to develop
Of which you hold a dream?
Or are those spots left vacant
With no future to redeem?

And when the storms arrive
Snow, wind, hail and even rain
How do you see what you have lost
As lack or a new plant to gain?

We're responsible for our own garden
Like we are for our own life
No one can choose what we plant
Or how we view our strife

So, tend to your garden thoughtfully
There're consequences for every choice
Be mindful of what you bring into it
Then sit back, take it in and rejoice!

The Lessons from the Redwoods

To stand beneath the Redwoods, where do I begin?
Its energy expansive, its knowledge held within
So much it holds to teach us, if we just observe and see
There's so much more to it, than being just a tree

Its height is quite impressive as it reaches for the sun
It shakes hands with the moon, when each new day is done
"The sky is the limit," I hear it gently say
As the breeze so lightly blows, and its branches start to sway

Its girth holds all the records, its circumference is quite grand
Each ring records the history, what has happened on this land
It's estimated age 1,500 years to date
I'm glad that I could visit before it was too late

Its canopy above provides cover overhead
It shelters those below, the shade it casts is so widespread
But through the leaves the sun, finds it's way upon the ground
I soak in all Its warmth, makes me feel all safe and sound

Its bark is thick and cracked, it has weathered all the storms
It teaches me the years, my exterior will form
But also that the storms, will not prevent my growth
I will carry this new message as my guide and my new oath

Its roots they do run deep, to support this large a frame
It connects to all the others, what a forest it became
So many, many things, for us to learn if we look deeper
The Redwoods are quite special; in this world they are a keeper!

The Canvas Lies Above

As I drive out of the city, the day is now complete
Destination is due north, warmers turned on in my seat
My mind is still a racing, but my breaths do start to slow
The music helps to lift me, the week's baggage I won't tow

City lights do fade away, but the stars light up the sky
They seem to be much brighter, and not in short supply
On occasion there's a cloud, that will hide a star or two
The wind blows them all along, my mood it can't subdue

I pull over and step out, to admire what lies above
There's a peace that fills my soul, like a gift dropped from a dove
The vastness it goes on, makes me pause in gratitude
To think I'm a small piece, in this heavenly solitude

Each star has contribution, to the view I'm taking in
Collectively they shine, on my face I wear a grin
To see a constellation is remarkable it's true
But to see them all together, is something to pursue

The glow each star puts forth, varied intensity and size
Unlike stadium lights, lined up in rows that burn our eyes
The variety on this canvas, is what makes me stand in awe
Luck may follow if you witness, shooting stars that God does draw

I believe we all are stars in life's canvas that we weave
Our differences important to the whole picture, I believe
I don't think stars above, try to outshine the glowing moon
All together there's a masterpiece, morning does come all too soon

And yes there will be clouds in our life from time to time
That may cover up our glow, that's when winds work overtime
For nothing can extinguish, the light that you were given
I hope you see the sky, above these roads that I have driven

Life is About Balance

Everything in nature has an equal and opposite energy. Everything. So
many examples we know. As within, so without; as above, so below;
yin-yang; sun-moon; light-dark; life-death; north-south; east-west; right-wrong;
protons-electrons; good-evil; men-women; old-young…
The list is endless.

Which gets me to thinking…have we ever considered the Divine
Masculine Energy? I believe that would be evident in Jesus. And doesn't
there also exist an equal and opposite energy known as the Divine
Feminine Energy? I believe that soul to be Mary Magdelene. Both
embodied love. Both were a shining example of how to walk this earth with
God's divine light. Both were messengers of God's Word. Both taught us in
the most humble way how to live according to God's plan. And when Jesus
gave His life and rose, it was Mary to whom He first revealed His risen soul. And
why wouldn't it be? She was His equal and opposite energy. She was
known as the apostle to the apostles.

Life is about balance. No side is better than the other. No side more
powerful than the other. When we embrace both sides of the coin, we
receive wealth. Not in a monetary way, but in the richness of life. A
partnership can achieve more than a single person if we empower each
other. Nothing exists in a vacuum without the opposing force. Learn to
recognize and embrace both sides. There is something good in everything.
Seek and you shall find. It's all about balance.

Chapter Eight

Discovering Purpose

This chapter reflects on finding meaning in life's moments. Poems like *Life's Key* and *Enjoy Your Vacation* see unpredictability as a path for growth, while *Graduation* and *End Times* highlight transformation and renewal. Metaphors like *To Thank a Gardener* emphasize cultivating a purposeful, fulfilling life by aligning values, faith, and intentionality.

Life's Key

God approached the group of twenty with a plan to help them see
As He watched them with their struggles to attempt to find life's key
I've placed the key high on the trees, to reach, a ladder just won't do
It requires you work in groups of four and devise a plan or two

The professions in the group were diverse as they could be
Bankers, architects, builders and artists sized up their tree
They formed the five groups needed, each working with like minds
The last to be picked in each of the jobs joined together, their rejection did bind

They set out to build a tree house, one that would reach up to the stars
Each feeling they would conquer the key, with their knowledge from seminars
The bankers had plenty of money to complete this simple task
The architects devised the plans, no help would be needed to ask

The builders held all the knowledge in making their structure secure
The artists would bring in design, its beauty they would procure
The misfit group had all of the talents it needed to be a success
And proved to be the best tree house, the height reached, it did impress

As they sat inside their tree house, filled with exhaustion, fulfillment and pride
They still could not locate the key, and believed possibly God may have lied
The key was in the journey, where lessons were revealed
It's not found by using a key to unlock a door where concealed

You learned that working with others, that have many a similar skill
Didn't prove to be the best choice, all the tasks it did not fulfill
I gave you each a talent, for life as you embark
Each person is just as important, to feel less is part of the dark

While it's comfortable to have others, agree with your every thought in life
It doesn't challenge you to grow and your life's safety creates no strife
It is during these challenges, that you all will learn the most
I promise it's more rewarding, than if through life you coast

Stop the judgment and work together, with others who aren't like your kind.
Your successes will be bigger and true happiness you will find.
I made you all to be different, each challenge a skill will require.
You'll learn solutions from others and achieve all your hearts desire

So love your fellow neighbor, embrace whatever their gift.
And help others around you, use your talents to give them a lift.
I hope you now get what I wanted, what I'm trying to get you to see.
The goal is love and acceptance, it's not found in a simple key

Enjoy Your Vacation

Vacation was upon us, relaxation now in sight
Would we decide to drive, or should we take a flight?
Our time off was approved, our bags had all been packed
There is nothing left to do at work, and nothing that we lacked

We thought about our journey, just how and where we'd travel
Would our roads all be paved, or would some turn out gravel?
Would we travel at high speed, or would we take our time?
Would our highways all be flat, or are there mountains we will climb?

Will we drive in a straight line, or will there be some bends
Would we take in all the scenery, of which God's artwork lends
And will our chosen path, be the same as others choose
Or will our choice of roads we take, cause us to blow a fuse?

Will we find some dead-end roads, that cause us to turn around
Would it have happened for a reason, a new adventure to be found
Or is it meant to teach us something we could then apply
To our next course decision, saved from danger that's nearby

It seems that such a trip, can resemble much in life
We choose our destination, but the path may cause us strife
And we may be required to turn around a time or two
We pray the journeys joyful, and our frustrations number few

To be less judgmental, something we should all strive for
The roads some choose to take, we might find a bore
There is no golden route, in this place that we do live
It seems each chosen path will have blessings it will give

Where we aspire to be, may also differ some
Each choice has repercussions, where our lessons all come from
So get excited for your journey, investigate your route
Turn to God when you hit detours, He'll help you out of doubt

What Does Graduation Mean?

We all attend schools in life, its attendance mandatory
The things that do take place there, help us write our story
Each grade teaches new lessons, and we then will take a test
And if we choose to pass them, we'll move on with all the rest

There are many teachers and mentors, who will help along the way
Their lessons will burn deeply, in our minds they're sure to stay
Most of them will guide us, and make us smarter pupils
And some of them cause scars, where it's pain in life quadruples

We learn to not make fun, of the younger grades below
But to help them through the journey, our knowledge to bestow
The subjects we excel in, will always vary much
Our gifts uniquely given, in everything we touch

And what will graduation mean, as you look back and reflect?
The chrysalis has opened; we now have wings we didn't expect
How will you all apply, the knowledge your mind now obtained?
Will you fly to new dimensions, limitations not restrained?

Let's take a deeper look, and consider something more
Imagine earth a school, where our souls come to restore
What lessons do we learn here, to connect with the divine?
Does graduation mean, that our hearts do now align?

We've all heard the old saying, "As above, so below"
Does it contain a message, that we should surely know
And where do we find guidance, as sometimes we'll trip and fall
I think we should look up, to where the stars do sprawl

It seems God does use stars, to help us light our way
And if we understand, on our path we'll surely stay
It worked for the three wise men, as they followed the brightest one
It led them to the solution that we now call, God's true Son

To Thank a Gardener

To grow a plant to beauty, requires a thing or two
It starts with a small seedling, placed below a sky so blue
In a bed of soil are nutrients, that will feed it as it grows
The height that it will get to, at first nobody knows

It will need to have some rain, through the roots it will then run
And occasional fertilizer, helps it reach up to the sun
Sometimes it needs transplanting, a different sort of spot
And pruning seems to aid it, cut away the dying rot

Some will need a trellis, to support it as it grows
And a few kind words will help it, when it looks a little low
If we attend to all its needs, a full bloom will then reveal
More than one or two we see, would really be ideal

We are like plants and all other living things
Who made you as a seedling, what safe harbor did they bring?
Who fed you food and water, that helped your body grow
Who nurtured your small spirit that from within did flow

Did you ever have a circumstance, that sprung from you new life?
Like a little fertilizer, though it felt like pain and strife
Was the pruning you received, full of joy or did it sting?
It all was necessary, your strength it did thus bring

And who would speak the kind words, when your mood was down and out
Did their hug feel like a trellis, to support you in that bout?
Were you brought outside to play, to feel the dirt and rain?
Did it bring new growth inside, stress from your body drain?

Were you moved to new locations, to offer you new roots?
Did it give you opportunities and one or two new shoots?
I'm hoping you were raised in the light of God and sun
And your beauty was full bloom when your life was said and done

So thank the gardener in your life, who attended all your needs
They were quite skilled in growing you, you started from small seeds
Don't do it with your words, as they don't really need to hear
To watch you bloom and grow, is what they hold most dear

The Sum of All Parts

A garden is not created, with attention to one seed
It takes soil, rain and sunlight to produce, each one a need
And the gardener is the one, who oversees all moving parts
To make sure they are in balance, so plants thrive and growing starts

The weather is not predicted, by just looking at a cloud
There are patterns, winds and fronts, their very nature can be loud
The meteorologist gathers all the science that's presented
Evaluates the trends, then the forecast is documented

The astrologer makes predictions, not just by looking at the moon
The sun and planets are involved, 'round each other move in tune'
The stars create the patterns, a map throughout the night
When pictured all together, there's a story that's in sight

The football games not won, with just the quarterback
They need offense and defense, evaluate plays they do lack
It takes the coach to guide them, from the sideline as they play
If a trophy they desire, and to the end they want to stay

So why are we surprised, when health care is not the best
Fragmented, different specialists, few internists guide the tests
They each stay in their lane, their body part they do assess
Hand you another pill, with a new bill you will possess

But who adds all the pieces, like the docs from days of old
What is this type of healthcare, what bill of goods have we been sold
And do all these prescriptions, ever take away the ill
Or do they hide our symptoms, and the cause remains there still

Who acts as the gardener, meteorologist, astrologer, and coach
Is there anyone in healthcare that uses this approach
Its my belief that looking back, to things we knew back then
Combined with our new knowledge, returns health to us again

Along the Country Road

The road winds on for miles, I move past in meditation
Off to both sides I see, the fields of vegetation
The rows are neatly planted, long days they did put forth
High yield anticipated, I continue to drive north

The fields appear symmetric, no weeds within are found
Likely due to poisons sprayed, upon this sacred ground
Winds blow across the crop, seems nature tries to rid
What wasn't present in the past, when I was just a kid

Once home I view my garden, not much order it contains
Weeds seem to grow much faster, as God brings sun and rains
My heart tells me be happy, with the food that's grown within
Though it isn't mass produced, to our bodies it won't sin

Mass plantings of the seeds, society does provide
May just contain some poison, to the farmers they have lied
More nutrition is not promised, as it's grown on this large scale
Profits shined above our food, and our health did start to fail

Take note of where your food is grown, don't worry bout the norm
If we learn from days of old, a better life will start to form
Don't be afraid to play in dirt, plant some seeds and watch them grow
Then enjoy a beverage in the chair upon the patio

What if it's not just about seeds, we plant in darkened dirt
But also ones within our brain, our thoughts need be alert
Don't be an eager beaver and believe what others do
Think for yourself then plant some seeds, even if just a few

End Times

We often hear of end times, the sound echoes in our ears
It leads us to anxiety, trepidation and our fears
To lose what we most value, from our comfort it would pull
What would it look like next, in our minds we start to mull

But why do we so fear, the ending of a chapter
As we usually turn the page, to read what does come after
Often times it's better, than the one preceding it
Yet we focus on the past, parts of it no longer fit

A caterpillar's life isn't sad when at the end
A butterfly is birthed, into the wind its wings do send
A graduation happens, at the end of education
Into the world we go, with new skills for integration

The pregnancy complete, gifts us a child of God
The wind and rain do stop, leaving rainbows o'er the sod
Our career we do retire, having worked so many years
To begin a great new chapter, our schedule finally clears

The ending of the day, leads to stillness, peace and rest
Tomorrow brings the dawn, when we are often at our best
So end times aren't all bad, as they usher in the new
Beginnings bring new blessings, leave behind what we outgrew

And when the end times come, for our time here on the earth
We'll shed our outer body, and our soul will see new birth
We never really end, we truly just change form
Where do you hold your focus, when life brings you through a storm?

Do You Look for the Flaw?

Life isn't perfect, but there's much to be grateful for
Sometimes we do forget this, and we're always seeking more
The things we have today, were once on our wish list
Do we appreciate, or forget that they exist

We've been groomed by our society, to focus on the lack
Overlook best parts of day, see the world in white or black
We focus on the bad grade, even though the rest are A's
We think about the mishaps, when performing in the plays

They forgot an anniversary, but each day treat you the best
We forget why we chose them, and in whose arms we want to rest
That car is sure a beauty, but did you notice the small dent
We had many conversations, but focus on one argument

We are dressed and look quite nice, but one hair is out of place
We've won many a hard game, but lost that one important race
We succeeded in so many ways at work, no room to fail
But do we focus on the challenge of the day, or the lost sale

The kids behaved so well, the majority of the day
Do we focus on the tantrum, when they were tired from the play
We checked many an item off, our list of things to do
But worry about the things we missed, that number one or two

We wake up every morning, move about and feel just fine
But when we come down with sickness, we feel free to cry and whine
And the dog who loves you at your worst, may have an accident inside
Is the carpet more important than the joy brought, you decide

When we choose to focus, on what's lacking in our life
We will sure find more examples, and to our days it will bring strife
But if you choose to focus on the good, you will find God
You will step off the dirt path, and rest upon the soft green sod

What Can You Spare?

So many natural disasters, so much need around the world
So many people hurting, as misfortunes round them swirled
And we may have escaped, the hardships that they face
But we are all connected, the entire human race

We need to help each other, in their despair we should all give
Help your neighbors when they struggle, it's a better way to live
But what if we can't help them, in a monetary way
What if what we have, is all used up by end of day

We will all experience, these short chapters in our life
And how to help another, when we are living our own strife
The good news is we've many ways, to help a person out
It's not always about money, it doesn't require clout

We can give them our attention, or a sympathetic ear
We can offer up a meal, or help them wipe a tear
Take care of a small child, or some elderly that day
Or sometimes a cup of coffee, and sit down with them and pray

Give someone a ride, who doesn't have a car
Borrow them a phone, to reach out to someone far
Help them with their medicine, do their laundry for the week
Help them with repairs, help find the answers they do seek

Take care of their pet, borrow a jacket and some boots
Pay them some respect, as their life puts down new roots
A bed that's nice and warm, out of storms for just a night
May help them level up, from their dreams chase out the fright

Worry not if you've no dollars and cents to spare
There's a lot of ways to give, to show others how you care
And when you do receive, all the rewards for working hard
You'll be able to give money, as your debt you do discard

We are all quite capable, of giving in all seasons
Hope and love are things to give, for a variety of reasons
To give is always better, than ever to receive
We are all in this together, this I truly do believe

What Are Your Priorities?

There's a natural wave to life, it seems to ebb and flow
There are times that seem too busy, others seem too slow
Things sometimes do expand, always followed by contraction
Appreciate them both, as they can lead to satisfaction

We've been gifted many resources, we often take for granted
We believe the roots that hold them, will retain as they were planted
We can fail to change our ways, when resources do diminish
Which can leave us in a bind, our assumptions hurt our finish

Our resources can be time, energy or our health
Or simply our attention, or the state of our wealth
And when it's slow to flow, our priorities become clear
We get crystal vision; on the things we hold most dear

These priorities are the things, we should be most grateful for
All other frills in life, enter through a second door
These are things for which we sacrifice, that make life worth the struggle
The things that we don't drop, when on our plate and we do juggle

Luckily the ebbs and contractions that occur
Only live in a chapter, a small section it does stir
Be grateful for these setbacks, as they clarify our vision
Use them as stepping stones, to the life you do envision

And take the needed steps when in abundance or in loss
Sometimes we build a bridge, other times we wait to cross
Look to your discernment, to know where you are at
Appreciate moving on, when no longer where you sat

It's sad we have gotten so busy, that priorities lost their rank
To not observe their value, until our lives began to sank
Try to combat this, live each moment in the now
And look to little children, who often show us how

The Secret of Life

The secret of life is no secret at all
It's to pass every test, whether it's big or it's small
It's to stay kind and humble and honest and real
And be empathetic to how others feel

It's to always treat others with grace and respect
Never cheat, lie or steal, our behavior, reflect
It's to never compare yourself with another
God made us all different, every sister and brother

We each have a purpose He gave to fulfill
With many a talent and many a skill
To discover them all can be quite a mission
But we have what we need to pass every lesson

It's to discover your passion and live to the fullest
It's there where your soul lives and where you'll find rest
And when life gives you trouble as it will often do
Ask, "What is my lesson?" Maybe it's one or it's two

For every challenge can make us rise higher
If we dig deep inside, keep our faith, never tire
It's to live your life with a grateful heart
Give thanks to God every day as we start

Be generous to others with all that you're given
Share and touch the lives that they may be living
To learn to forgive any wrongs done against you
To not hold a grudge and waste days that are few

Love the people in your life you've been given for your aide
They each are quite special, don't let memories fade
It's to own our choices, behavior, mistakes
Not project on another or make your truth fake

It's to accept God's timing and plans for our life
Not think we control it as it will cause strife
It's to choose faith over fear for our every day
Let life unfold naturally and our hearts with God stay

If we follow the simple guidelines above
We'll find our path easier and a life that we love
For this is what God had in mind for us
Not to complain and make life such a fuss

Our trip back to heaven will be full of glory
What life are you living to bring back as your story?

Author's Note

Life is a journey and each challenge offers us an opportunity for growth. God has guided my journey. My prayer is the things I learned along the way will aid you on your journey. These poems are examples of how God wants me to see the world. My hope is that the things I've learned may inspire you to look at life from a new perspective.

Thank you to my husband and children for walking this life with me and for their unending love and support. I am forever grateful for their encouragement to be my authentic self. A special thank you to Deja for helping these poems take flight.

About the Author

After retiring from a 34-year career as a general dentist with her own practice, Wendy Koury has been inspired to help people in a new way. Enjoying being married for 37 years, raising three children, and being a grandmother of two while working with beautiful families has given her a window into life struggles. God has guided her journey and now she is hoping to inspire others to contemplate their own experiences and find strength in life's ups and downs.